HIGH DAYS *and* HOLY DAYS

St. Paul's 2008:Years 7-13.

HIGH DAYS *and* HOLY DAYS

A History of St Paul's School for Girls

Jean Simpson

BREWIN BOOKS

First published by
Brewin Books Ltd, 56 Alcester Road,
Studley, Warwickshire B80 7LG in 2008
www.brewinbooks.com

ISBN: 978-1-85858-425-6 (Paperback)
ISBN: 978-1-85858-424-9 (Hardback)

A Cataloguing in Publication Record
for this title is available from the British Library.

Typeset in Bembo
Printed in Great Britain by
The Alden Press.

CONTENTS

ACKNOWLEDGMENTS

Thanks are due to a very great number of past and present pupils and staff: especially to Mary Holland, Philippa Jordan, Teresa Monteiro and Gill Methley-Smith (who sadly died before completion of the project) who have been involved with the history for a number of years; also to Beverly Chapple, Claire Eastwood, Kathleen and Monica Hermolle, Margaret Wilson, Roger Browning and all the many others who contributed memories of their time at St. Paul's.

I am most grateful to Angela Whelan and Maureen May for their support, encouragement and assistance with proof reading and checking.

Particular thanks must go to Sister Hilary, the moving force behind the project and an inexhaustible source of inspiration and information, who has been tireless in contacting former staff and pupils, and in checking drafts. Any errors and oversights are solely the responsibility of the author; please accept her regrets and apologies for the same, and good wishes to all readers of this centenary history, and to St. Paul's for the next hundred years.

FOREWORD

By Sr. Thérèse Browne, Superior General,
Congregation of the Sisters of Charity of St. Paul the Apostle.

In the centenary year of St. Paul's School for Girls I welcome the opportunity to write the Foreword to *High Days and Holy Days*.

This book, one of the gifts of the school's centenary celebrations, is no mere chronicle of historical events. Instead, the author has created a record of a vibrant school community by drawing on personal memories from a variety of sources.

The school, founded by the Sisters of Charity of St. Paul, the Apostle, has always maintained a strong sense of its Mission to provide a Catholic education for Girls in Birmingham.

For the Sisters to undertake such a major project in 1908 required a strong faith, with no small measure of courage, generosity and self-sacrifice to provide the necessary resources. It is, however, an indication of what can be achieved by a Community trying to meet a real need, convinced of the dignity of every person and the value of a faith based education for the common good.

Upholding traditional values and standards while embracing the best of educational initiatives is a consistent thread that runs through St. Paul's one hundred year history. This is due in no small measure to the faith, dedication, stability and creativity of the leadership given by successive Governing Bodies, Headteachers and Staff over the years, together with the presence and support of the Sisters.

The School community has been enriched in many ways by the increasing cultural diversity among its members. Its on-going professional, curriculum and faith development owes much to its successful collaboration with the Archdiocese of Birmingham, the Local Education Authority, Birmingham's Catholic Schools Partnership and the wider local community. The school's outreach programmes of support for charitable causes together with its expanding national and international educational network are impressive to say the least.

May St. Paul's School for Girls go forward into the 21st century living what it always knew in its daily routines, namely that every member of its community matters. May it continue to be a beacon of educational excellence preparing young women to take their place as responsible members of their families and their faith communities, good citizens always ready to be of service to society, especially those in need.

Chapter 1

THE BEGINNINGS (1908–1923)

7th October, 1908, in Vernon Road, Edgbaston; a mid-autumn day, no doubt with the leaves falling in a road leafy then as now. There were not, perhaps, so many houses in the street then, though a fair number of them date from the late Victorian and Edwardian period. No convent then, with its grand campanile and imposing chapel roof – but the admiration of every eye would surely have been the new school building, handsome in its red brick with light stone facings and topped with the graceful cupola,

St. Paul's High School, 1908.

shining in the autumn sun. Those who explored further would have seen the spacious grounds leading down to the reservoir, which then apparently reached almost to the railings bordering the field – a much larger expanse of water than there is now.

On that October day, there was a particular stir and bustle in the road with numerous cabs and carriages arriving. Even one or two motor cars were noticed. The occasion was the opening ceremony of St. Paul's High School, where lessons had started about a month earlier. That previous informal opening day had apparently been postponed by a week, as the building was not quite finished (plus ça change?)

The building's foundation stone had been laid on December 17th, 1907, as reported in the Catholic Gazette of that week.

"The Bishop blessed, and the Duke of Norfolk laid the foundation stone of the new Secondary School and Pupil Teachers' Centre in Vernon Road, Edgbaston. It is intended to accommodate 237 pupils in three departments: High School, 157, Pupil Teachers' department, 50, Kindergarten, 30. The Lord Mayor and a number of the City council were present. The total cost, including the cost of site, will fall not far short of £20,000. The offerings on the stone amounted to £165."

Top: Front Doorway.
Bottom: The Hockey Field in winter.

In August, the first teachers and pupils had moved into No. 16 and 18 Vernon Road, the houses which served as home for the sisters/teachers and pupil boarders, before the eventual building of the convent next to the school. The sisters were Mother Emelia, Sr. Victorine, Sr. Carthage and Sister St. Thérèse, soon to be joined by about 15 boarders from Ireland. The latter, aged between 15 and 17, were all prospective or "pupil" teachers attached to various Catholic Elementary schools throughout the city of Birmingham for training. These "apprentice" teachers, day students as well as boarders formed the nucleus of the pupils in the beginning, but were soon to be joined by others not necessarily destined to teach. The school opened with about 100 pupils.

The background to the building of the school and its opening with this emphasis on the training of Catholic teachers encompassed a number of factors. The most striking of these was the strong sense of mission and purpose of the Sisters of Charity of St. Paul. Added to this was the impetus given by the Education Act of 1902 to secondary education in general, and the consciousness of the Catholic Community in particular that "they would not allow their children to begin their career in the world less well-equipped than their fellows, nor could they allow them to be forced to such educational advantages in non-Catholic schools." (from the foreword to the Opening Day programme).

From September, 1901 there had existed a Catholic pupil-teacher centre, known as St. Paul's College, at No. 6 Whittall Street, close to the city centre. Its establishment had been one of the closing acts in the eventful life of Mother Genevieve Dupuis, foundress of the Congregation of the Sisters of Charity of St. Paul, who died in 1903. Whittall Street was in fact a boarding house for about 40 trainee teachers who were joined in the late afternoons and evenings by another 30 or so non-residents for classes at St. Chad's Girls' School. During the day they were learning the

Terms of reference for Committee of Management, 24th June 1907.

practical side of their future trade in the city's Catholic elementary schools like St. Chad's. They were taught mostly by the Sisters who were themselves the Heads of the elementary schools.

3

Left: Mother Genevieve Dupuis, 1813–1903. Foundress of the Congregation of the Sisters of Charity of St. Paul. Top right: Description of Foundation Stone, 17th December, 1907 by Mother Mechtilde Thelan (3rd Mother-General). Bottom right: Opening Ceremony Programme, 7th October 1908.

Not unusually for a St. Paul's institution, they impressed His Majesty's Inspectors of the day, one of whom, a Mr Ferand, urged that, based on the talents, good practice and results of the Whittall Street College, a secondary school should be founded. Later the same idea was espoused by the then Bishop Ilsley of Birmingham, who made an urgent request to the Sisters of St. Paul to "supply the long-felt need of a secondary school for the Catholic girls." The words are quoted by Mother Mechtilde Thelan, the fourth Mother-General of the Congregation, referring to his request in her letter to Bishop Ilsley the week before the official opening. The letter makes clear the energy and vision of the Sisters, determined, as their Superior says, to provide a

Letter from Mother Mechtilde to Bishop Ilsley re funding, October 1908.

school "worthy of this great city and district." It also reflects the spirit of sacrifice which will be familiar to all who know the Sisters, and the school. Mother Mechtilde points out that the total cost of the site, the buildings, furniture and equipment was close to £18,000, of which the Sisters were compelled to borrow a large portion. She continues, "our only means of liquidating the debt will be the savings of the earnings of the Sisters teaching in the elementary schools in many parts of England. Moreover, to provide this school we must indefinitely postpone the building for ourselves at the Mother House of a permanent Choir Chapel." In fact money already collected for the latter purpose was now diverted to meet some of the expenses of the new school.

The greatest burden then was to lie with the Sisters, with other monies coming from fees, Government grants and subscriptions from the better-off members of the Birmingham Catholic Community. The fees at that time were two guineas a term, though there was always consideration given by the Sisters to families who found it difficult to pay. The school began with a Secondary and a Pupil-teachers' Department, and a little later a Kindergarten was formed for girls and boys under eight.

The hundred or so pupils present on October 7th were probably outnumbered by the dignitaries and parents who arrived. The opening ceremony took place in the Central Hall (now known as the Old Hall). The magnificent plasterwork would have

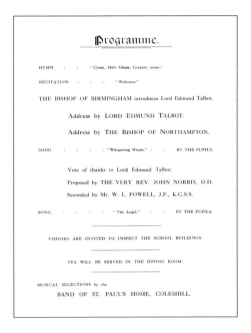

Opening Ceremony Programme, 7th October 1908.

been brand new, and the walls, now covered with medal and honour boards would have been bare and freshly painted. The Duke of Norfolk, England's premier Catholic aristocrat, had laid the foundation stone in 1907, but he was unable to attend through illness, and the ceremony was performed by Lord Edmund Talbot, who spoke enthusiastically of the new buildings as "a monument to the educational life of Birmingham", and appealed to all present to share in the financial burden borne so heavily by the Sisters of Charity of St. Paul. The Bishop of Northampton echoed his call for voluntary subscribers, pointing out that the cost of maintaining the school could not possibly be met by the fees and government grant received. The architect, Mr H.T. Sandy, presented Lord Talbot with a golden key, as a memento of the occasion.

And what of the pupils at the centre of it all? Dressed in white, they had stood on either side of the entrance hall, together with the staff, to welcome the guests, and according to the programme, had sung a hymn and two songs. The singers probably stood in the balcony, or Upper Corridor overlooking the Hall, as there was really no room for them downstairs. Certainly after entertaining the company they did not stay for the main part of the ceremony as they were sent off to the

Science Lecture Room. Writing in 1958, one recalled that they were left without a teacher, and simply told to be very quiet. "No child spoke or left her seat. I shall always remember that dead silence – such self-control. There were no books to read. We were simply told to be quiet, and we did as we were told. Maybe the silence lasted for an hour, but the memory of that obedience has lasted for fifty years." (recollected by Margaret McGillycuddy, writing in the Golden Jubilee magazine of 1958).

Early group of pupils, c. 1910.

Such self-discipline augured well for the founding of the School, and this was proved almost immediately by the success of the first full inspection which took place just one month after the official opening, in November, 1908. It is difficult to imagine a newly opened school nowadays facing its first OFSTED within two months of classes starting for the first time, but those were perhaps sterner times, and everyone must have been very conscious of the weight of expectation hanging on them. However, as the first Head, Mother Emelia recorded, "In due time a very gratifying report of the Full Inspection was received from the Government."

An early prospectus tells us that "the Course of Studies comprises all the branches of a solid English Education, to which are added Science, Latin, French, Drawing, Singing, the various kinds of needlework, Domestic Science, Physical

Edith Prince, Boarder, c. 1908.

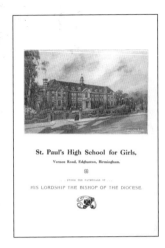

School Prospectus, 1909.

Exercises and Organised Games." In 1908, all the teachers were ladies, with about half a dozen lay staff (all unmarried, at that time when it was customary for a woman to give up employment on marriage), in addition to the Sisters who had come from Whittall Street with Mother Emelia.

Mother Emelia was clearly a memorable and inspiring character. She was Head from 1908 until 1923, and was variously described by her pupils as follows: "born to govern but her rule was wise and kind"; "a motherly bespectacled nun with a beaming smile"; "a strict disciplinarian and her training laid emphasis on good manners"; "a nun of impressive though kindly manner"; and "a welcome visitor in the classroom always." Some vivid pictures are presented in the recollections of those who knew her: an early memory is of Mother Emelia conducting rehearsals for the first Prize Day on July 22nd, 1909, with each and every pupil practising walking gracefully backward from the platform in case she was called up to receive an award, for, as Mother Emelia said, "A prize should be a surprise."

Another memory is of the Headmistress throwing wrapped caramels from the Balcony (i.e. the upper corridor above the Old Hall) to the pupils below, the more agile receiving the lion's share of the caramels!

Much later, on the news of the signing of the Armistice on November 11th, 1918, the then Cookery Mistress, Sister Perpetua, recalled Mother Emelia, "greatly excited", ringing not one but two bells, one in each hand, long and furiously, so that the girls all ran out of their classrooms to hear the news.

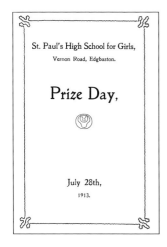

Prize Day Programme, July 1913.

By the time she retired at Christmas in 1922 Mother Emelia had moulded the school into a strong institution which already possessed a vigorous tradition and distinctive ethos. Apparently one of her favourite quotations was:

"Stone walls do not a prison make,

Nor iron bars a cage."

It is certain that under her firm but kindly direction the walls of St. Paul's High School were in fact a means of opening up a new world of learning, community and enjoyment which was fondly and gratefully remembered by that first generation of pupils.

Mother Emelia was not alone in creating an impression. Among the first teachers were Miss Mitchell, remembered for having miraculously produced "Cinderella" in French on the first Prize Day, two sisters, Miss Alice and Miss Edith Colley, who covered between them Latin, English, Maths and Science, Miss Rich who taught an interesting combination of Maths and Games, Miss Sheridan for History and Miss Smith, who taught the Art classes seated in the Hall to draw objects including cones and cylinders.

Sister Mary of the Cross (sometimes called "Smock", but not in her hearing) was clearly a character. Even in 2001, Mrs Agnes Robinson (née Deeley) vividly remembered her as a marvellous teacher, but a law unto herself. She started her Maths class at nine o'clock sharp, and apparently locked the door so that her class did not go into Assembly with the other girls, but did Maths instead. Others remember her as hiding a heart of gold beneath a stern exterior, and bringing success to "even the most unpromising of pupils."

Not surprisingly great excitement was occasioned by the news that a master, Mr Meixner, was to be appointed to teach Maths and Chemistry. He was to remain at the school until 1949, except for war service from 1914 to 1918. There are many recollections of Mr Meixner. He taught in a manner described as "staccato but excellent." Apparently though it was not impossible for the wilier (or naughtier) pupils to divert him by introducing the subject of the Boat Race, on which, as a Cambridge man, he could be led to discourse in a partisan way. As the sole male teacher for many years, he had his own staff room, described as a "cavern full of wreathing cigarette smoke." It was Mr Meixner who gave great encouragement to the founding of the Old Girls' Association and became its first President.

Many members of staff who came to the school in those early days were to remain in the school's service for most of their teaching careers. Such were Miss Jones, Miss Hughes, Miss Smith, Miss Mongey, Miss Bell, Miss Mayes and Miss Innes.

Miss Innes taught French from 1913 to 1953, and seems to have imprinted herself firmly in the recollections of the pupils she taught. She was described as "a dainty

A Drill Class in the Assembly Hall.

Science Lecture Room.

little person", and a brilliant teacher of French, but seems to have had something of a Gallic temperament to match, as one day she arrived at a Fourth Form lesson, stood in the doorway and pitched the homework books across the floor. She then left without ever having entered the classroom. In her earlier days she was also teacher of Physical Exercises, which pre-1920 consisted of walking along benches and jumping off, clad in full school uniform.

Either Miss Bell (Maths and History) or Miss Eagle (English and History) had round rubber heel protectors screwed onto her black boots, which squeaked as the teacher strode through the corridors.

Miss Eagle was evidently very popular; she arrived in 1922 and is remembered as being the nearest of the staff in age to the girls, and the most approachable. She seems to have been a young woman of great sincerity and earnestness who was pictured in memory as "marching through the corridors, her head invariably thrust forward and in her arms a pile of books." It was she who introduced the Society of the Holy Childhood, which was taken up by the girls with enthusiasm. They charted the progress of children in Africa, and this led to a link with a native school at Embakwe in what was then Southern Rhodesia.

Miss Eagle remained however only ten years at St. Paul's. In 1932 she entered the Redemptoristine Convent at Chudleigh, carrying with her "the affection and gratitude of the pupils", as recorded in the school journal of events in 1933.

The dedicated and often lengthy service of such committed teachers provided inspiration and a sense of continuity which is very evident in the recollections of many Old Girls. It has indeed been a feature of St. Paul's throughout its history.

THE CHOIR AND FATHER ROBERT EATON

St. Paul's has a long and outstanding musical tradition. No account of the school's early days would be complete without mention of Father Robert Eaton's famous choir.

Mother Emelia was apparently the inspiration behind its existence, having been dissatisfied with the Prize Day entertainment in 1910, and determined that there should be a really good concert the following year. But the chief moving spirit of the Choir was Father Robert Eaton of the Oratory, who taught Scripture and Music at St. Paul's on two afternoons each week,

Top: Portion of the Dining Hall.
Centre: The Kitchen.
Bottom: Portion of a Form Room.

and was from 1911 to 1927 the conductor of the School Choir. Practice was always on Saturday afternoons from two o'clock to three thirty, a sacrifice of free time apparently eagerly made, to judge from the fact that there were said hardly ever to have been absences. There were about forty singers.

Laboratory with Form VI.

Writing in 1958, Sister Thérèse Marie (Catherine Monaghan) remembered the intensity of the experience. "How we shivered with apprehension at the anticipation of those dreaded sight-reading tests, but how we thrilled to the harmony of the "Lovely stuff! Lovely stuff!" so lavishly provided. Which of us can ever forget him, as with voice, piano and violin, he carried us away into a new world."

The choir became known for a remarkable record of success at the Midland Musical Competition Festival, beginning in 1912. As the years went by they won prizes, banners and admiration as far afield as Leamington, Malvern and Tewkesbury. These were occasions not only of musical achievement but a chance for a good day out, perhaps even with a picnic or a row on the River Severn.

The singers on these red-letter days were resplendent in white dresses. One year they were winners at each of three big Midland festivals and were awarded silk banners, which floated proudly in the School Hall; one having been marched in triumph through the city streets from the station by the joyful winners.

Father Robert clearly demanded perfection from his singers – and got it! As one recollected, "he seemed to draw our voices as on invisible strings to one lovely sound." His own favourite instrument was the violin, which he would use at choir practice to demonstrate how he wanted a particular phrase to be sung.

His niece, Miss Sybil Eaton, was also a talented violinist, and it was regarded by the girls as a particular treat when Father Robert brought her to school to give a recital, not least because time was given from lessons to listen to the music.

Later on, Father Robert's indispensable partner was Miss Winifred Mayes, who accompanied the choir on the piano, and eventually took over the baton when he retired. She was a former pupil and choir member who became teacher of Music and Singing at St. Paul's, a post she held for many years. She and Father Robert clearly made an excellent team, and he wrote in 1933, "The work of the Choir is safe in her hands."

Top: The Entrance corridor.
Bottom: Original Building.

Chapter 2

BRANCHING OUT (1923–1939)

In January 1923, pupils returned to school to be greeted by a new Headmistress, Sister Veronica, who would in fact be in charge of the school until 1959, and who remains the longest-serving Head to date. In March, His Majesty's Inspectors came to the school. A pupil at the time recollected an inspector's visit to Miss Eagle's History lesson, the subject of which was the quarrel between Henry II and Archbishop Thomas Becket. An argument regarding the different viewpoints of Church and State ensued, continuing until well after four o'clock! The inspector was amused and said they were a lively class. Not surprisingly, if this was a typical visit, the school came through once again with flying colours. Change and development from then on seem to have been the hallmark of this period.

It was noted that the number of pupils had more than doubled since the previous inspection in 1914, and accordingly a new block of four classrooms was added in September, 1924. The system for Intending Teachers was also changed around this time, with a Bursary system replacing the old Pupil-teacher training system. This meant that the school had a permanent Sixth Form, the curriculum for which was widened in 1927 when there was no longer any difference between the school education of intending teachers and others.

In 1927 a House system was introduced, and survived into the early 1970s. The Silver Jubilee Magazine of 1933 includes a description for each house of its patroness: St. Agnes (yellow), St. Joan (the red ones), St. Theresa of Lisieux (green), and Our Lady of Loreto (blue). The House Reports in the same magazine suggest how strongly the system permeated school life, far beyond the sports field. There were House trophies for Study and for Order. There is a lively account from Loreto House of how they determined to make a bid for the Study Trophy, spurred on by a rousing address from their Housemistress. There followed "a ding–dong battle between Loreto and St. Joan's", culminating in a victory for Loreto, among whose members the name of M. Seeney stood out as having gained more than 50 marks to her credit in several months. Nor was it all hard work in the classroom or games field; each house celebrated the feast of its Patron in various enjoyable ways, including a Fancy Dress Ball for Loreto (which even succeeded in raising a slight profit), and a visit to Cadbury's for St. Joan's, with a tour of the "Factory in a Garden" in the firm's own char-a-banc and a tea, naturally together with sample chocolates! In 1936, Eileen Hemus (Mrs Shaw) recalls, "we were given chocolates in a presentation box to commemorate the Silver Jubilee of King George V. They were made of tin and all of us used them as pencil boxes, but when they fell to the floor they made an awful clatter, so we were stopped from using them."

Netball Team and Miss Troughton.

One area of school activity which really seems to have taken off in the 1920s was Physical Education. When a new P.E. mistress, Miss McCullagh arrived, the rather decorous exercises performed on the bench under the direction of Miss Innes were replaced by much more progressive activities. In the words of Theresa Gay (later Mrs Priest), "Miss McCullagh inverted us instead of the benches." This was controversial – parents wrote indignant letters, and some pupils invented ingenious excuses but still they had to stand on their heads. Soon a new teacher, Miss Hirst, arrived with further innovations. She was succeeded in 1925 by Miss Eileen Troughton, who had been trained at Bedford P.E. College, and soon built up successful teams in hockey and netball, as well as introducing Greek and National dancing, of which the girls gave several displays. Miss Troughton was considered to be very smart, especially when she wore a smocked blouse, pleated gym dress and leather gym 'pumps'. She had a great influence on her pupils, several of whom went on to teach or demonstrate the new

Lay Staff, 1926.

17

Form VI, 1922–23.

'gymnastics'. Eventually Miss Troughton married and became Mrs Harper. She then
went on to become the first woman Principal of the Birmingham Athletic Institute.

The Hockey Club of this era ran their own selection committee meetings,
usually in a café in town, fuelled with coffee and buns. For five successive years from
1928 to 1932 the school won the Birmingham and District Netball Shield, and was
winning 75% of its matches in hockey, cricket and tennis.

Eileen Hemus recalls playing tennis and cricket in the summer, and in the winter
netball and hockey. "If you were lucky enough to get into the school team you were
allowed to wear a yellow and navy girdle, instead of the navy one. I eventually gained
one for netball. Sports Day was quite an occasion and we had various races including
the 'plant pot' race, when you had to stand on two pots and then balance on one leg,
move the pot forward in front of you and stand on that and then move the one
behind you to the front and so progress to the finish (if you were lucky!)"

Other activities flourished. The School Magazine of 1938 records that the
previous year Sister Veronica had suggested the formation of a school Dramatic
Society. Enthusiasm was such that two societies were formed, one meeting on a

Kindergarten, 1922.

Wednesday and one on a Thursday. A number of plays were read, and at the end of term each group would present a play to the other.

Two parts of the school which lent St. Paul's special character at this time were the Preparatory Department and the Boarding Houses across Vernon Road.

There was a Kindergarten and a Preparatory Department from the very early days of the school, admitting both boys up to the age of eight, and girls from the age of five until eleven, when they could take the Ordinary Entrance Examination of the city, and girls could then pass into the Secondary Department; in the 1930s the average number of pupils doing so was about ten each year.

Former Kindergarten pupils have fond memories of the Sisters who taught them, including Sisters Annunciata, Gonzaga, Magdalen, Maria and Sylvester. The latter "made school a happy place. How we loved to get her off the subject and onto her own mischievous youth." (Dympna Morby). Other memories are of the percussion band (with the boys having priority over the drums!) and of working on slates with white chalk for Maths. Sister Annunciata read stories from the Old Testament, and later Sister Magdalen would prepare pupils for their first Holy Communion.

St. Paul's Choir, March 1929 (with Miss Mayes).

Memories of the Preparatory Department seem universally to be of carefree days before the pressures of the "Big School" took over.

Most of the Sisters who taught in the preparatory department are also very present in the recollections of the boarders of this period. In the days before the present Convent was built, most of the teaching Sisters lived in the house opposite the school at No. 16 Vernon Road, with the upstairs front room as the Chapel. No. 18 was the house for the boarders, and their number was limited by the amount of beds that could be squeezed into the black and white house. It was usually in the region of 24 to 28. Writing in 1958, Marie Derbyshire (Mrs Fussell) vividly recalled her experiences twenty years earlier under the watchful eye of Sister Magdalen, the rattling of whose rosary was the first and last sound of her day. She also recalled mastering the art of pleating the white curtains which separated their cubicles, appealing to Sister Joseph, the laundry Sister for lost handkerchiefs, and "tonsillitis in the sickroom with the fire burning and dear Sister Marie spoiling me."

The boarders' experiences of weekends were of Saturday mornings devoted to shoe cleaning in the Boot Room, and sweeping and tidying their dormitories. Sundays could not exactly have been considered as days of rest, for the journey to

Outing to Brewood, 1937.

Mass at the Oratory was not by the short direct route. Instead, presumably so that they would have used up too much energy to fidget during the service, the girls assembled at half-past nine and were marched down Vernon Road, up Rotton Park Road and then via Norfolk Road, Nursery Road, Somerset Road as far as Richmond Hill Road, and then eventually back to Hagley Road and so into the gallery of the Oratory. They stayed there for the High Mass at 10.45 and on until after the sermon given as part of the twelve o'clock Mass, after which they crept down the stone stairs and back (by the direct route!) for lunch at one o'clock in Vernon Road. Should anyone have fidgeted (or perhaps nodded off after all that walking) one of the Sisters sitting behind had her brolly on hand to poke the inattentive.

The best day of the year for the boarders was Corpus Christi. Then, dressed in their cotton frocks (of which each girl had just one) they were taken by taxi to the Mother House in Selly Park. Their white dresses, kept for processions, went ahead of them, and they changed into them for the Mass and procession round the Convent gardens. They were given buns and milk from the Convent's own cows. Then, back in cotton dresses, they were escorted by some of the Sisters to the tram terminus at Rednal. Here they were given a bag of sandwiches and a shilling piece, and set free till 5.30. The shillings were generally spent at Jose Collins's funfair, on merry-go-round rides and hooplas. The Sisters always knew where to find them, and they returned to Vernon Road on the tram, invariably with noses and arms burning from the sun. "Strange," recalled Audrey Worrall (Mrs Wardell), writing in 1988, "but in all those nine years (i.e. 1924–1932) I cannot recall that Feast Day being rainy."

Pilgrimage to Lourdes, 1939.

Just before the Second World War the present Convent was built in Vernon Road, with provision for boarders. However on the outbreak of war the boarders, along with most of the rest of the school, were evacuated to Hereford. Before the end of the war the 1944 Education Act had been passed and one of the consequences was that the Preparatory Department became a separate school, housed in the classrooms in the new Convent. There it continued until 1961. There were never again any boarders, but their recollections form a lively part of the school's history, and warmly attest to the motherly care given them by the Sisters in those two houses which still stand just across Vernon Road.

Chapter 3

THE OLD GIRLS' ASSOCIATION

Mrs Agnes Lambert (née Ward) wrote the following account at the time of the School's eightieth anniversary.

"In Summer, 1917, Kathleen Hawkins and I borrowed Mother Emelia's files, and sent out about eighty letters to local past students of St. Paul's, to which we had about forty replies to our first meeting.

"We held three meetings a year, about mid-term, and always had an item of interest – an Old Girl singer, an Old Girl of repute giving a talk, piano duets or quartets, etc. I have always supported Sue Ryder's wonderful work, so for one meeting every member brought an article for sale at one of her shops.

"A discussion group was formed with Joan Ireson in charge, and about twenty members met once a month at the school – most enjoyable.

"With Father Robert Eaton as conductor, a choir was formed of about thirty members, following on from the wonderful choir we had with him at school. This formed the nucleus of the Catholic Choir later on.

"About 1923 two hockey teams were formed, and we played any local teams, mostly from firms, who would have us. The home games were at school, with tea in the dining room afterwards.

"Several of us had brothers at St. Philip's, and the Oratory Cricket Club; we combined for dances in St. Philip's Hall (flannel dances in the summer) and a good time was had by all, including at one famous Ball at Edgbaston Assembly Rooms.

"The Association kept going during the war with difficulty and decreased numbers, but emerged again later. Mr Meixner, our Maths master, was our Chairman for many years and was very popular.

"On the School's Silver Jubilee, a large sit-down supper was arranged in the School Hall; on the Golden Jubilee a grand buffet supper was provided.

"The Annual Requiem Mass was inaugurated at the Golden Jubilee in 1958 when funds were raised to provide for the annual mass in perpetuity. This was at the suggestion of Mrs Theresa Jordan (née McCann) the mother of our own Miss Philippa Jordan."

The minutes of the Old Girls' Association record its continuing history, generally with a small core of faithful members who sometimes had to struggle to keep going in the face of small numbers and consequently rocky finances. Dances, concerts, talks and theatre trips were organised with varying degrees of support. Much heart searching was done over ways to attract new members, especially of a younger age group; perhaps however it is a fact of life that the years of youth are so full of activity that there is little room for nostalgia and it is only in middle age (or sometimes later!) that the desire to meet old school friends and share old memories is awakened. There were perennial discussions over the question of raising the subscription: in 1962 it was agreed that subscriptions should remain at 2/6, as they had been for a number of years, but "appeals should be made for those who can afford more to contribute something to postal expenses." In 1964 the committee gave way to inflationary pressure and the subscription was raised to 5/-.

Also in the early 1960s, an Old Girls' Association scarf was stocked by Moss Bros in Temple Street, priced at 27/6. After much discussion and submission of various designs, this was replaced in 1962 by a silk square at 29/11. This appears to have been superseded as a souvenir by the St. Paul's mugs of the 1990s which are still available, together with a new centenary design.

Theatre trips to Stratford were popular in the 50s but by the 1960s they were apt to sustain losses as a block of tickets had to be purchased when the booking season opened, but members either dropped out or wanted to travel by car when a coach had been booked and paid for. Nevertheless there were usually three meetings each year, at which often talks were given, sometimes by Old Girls on their careers in various parts of the world, or on various aspects of Catholic life and work. Sometimes there was a programme of music and dance by the present pupils. In the 1970s a tradition began of having a lunch or buffet in June, to coincide with the feast of SS. Peter and Paul. The Annual General meeting is held in October, along with the Mass inaugurated at the Golden Jubilee. Throughout the minutes of the Association, though, there have been continued calls for a substantial part of meetings to be devoted simply to an opportunity for chat and "catching up", which most members see as the main reason for membership. The success of this approach is amply illustrated by the decibel level as the Hall fills up with ladies of all ages chattering with the vivacity of schoolgirls.

The Association has been served with great dedication by its various committees and officials over the years. Notable names among these include Dympna Morby, Mary Whitwell, Sheila Smith (née Realfe), Wendy Cleary and the present Chair, Anne Russell (née Whelan).

Throughout the life of the Old Girls' Association, fund-raising has taken place, both for charitable causes and to help the school itself, most notably at times when extra money was badly needed to support new building work, after the fire of 1973, and during the various extensions. The Association has been very active in supporting the charities espoused by the school itself, including Father Hudson's Homes, work in Romania, the Fireside project, and latterly Freedom Park, the AIDS and HIV squatter camp in South Africa.

In 2008, June will see a special celebration weekend for the Old Girls' Association, to mark the school's centenary. No doubt this will attract a larger number than usual to revisit the school, and marvel at all the changes while recognising old haunts and chatting over memories. The actual centenary for the Association itself will not come until 2017, by which time another whole generation of St. Paul's Girls will have qualified to join its ranks. The growth of the internet has revivified many former students' associations, and there is no reason to suppose St. Paul's will be different. No matter how active or otherwise its members, they will be part of a network which is truly worldwide.

Chapter 4

ST. PAUL'S AT WAR (1939–1945)

On September 1st, 1939, 161 pupils were evacuated to Hereford. This was not the whole school, as some parents decided that they did not want their families to be split up, or as one mother said, "Better if we are all annihilated together!" For those who departed on the train from New Street Station, it was however a real adventure, since they were not told where they were going (the first of many lessons that "careless talk costs lives.") When they arrived at Hereford they were billeted in local households. This took longer in some cases than others: Margaret O'Connor recalled trudging up and down streets with her gas-mask and suitcase after finding the family she had been allocated to had mysteriously acquired a lodger, after being informed that a child was to be billeted on them. She was the last child left, and just as it seemed there was no room for her anywhere a woman stepped out of her house, which was already full, and said she could not bear to see her in this plight and would take her in.

At first the pupils were set to help with the hop-picking, earning, as Dympna Morby (née Taylor) recalls, "money, grimy hands and a passing acquaintance with members of the Romany tribe," as they helped to save the nation's beer. By the end of September a scheme had been worked out whereby St. Paul's shared the premises of the local Girls' High School, attending on Tuesdays, Thursdays and Saturdays. Many of the teachers had to return to Edgbaston every few days to teach or to set work for the few girls whose parents had not wished them to be evacuated. A "Correspondence School" was formed for non-evacuees who received in the post large envelopes with questions and exercises to be completed weekly. Joyce Harler (Mrs Fisher) was one such. She remembers that it was a novelty to work at home, and that the girls "played fair and did the work."

Those were the days of the "phoney" war, and after six months the evacuees returned to Birmingham. School re-opened at Vernon Road on February 27th, 1940, with 221 Secondary and 45 Preparatory pupils attending. Blast-diverting walls, wire netting on windows and sandbags were in place for air raid protection. An RAF unit had taken possession of most of the games field with their barrage balloon. In fact the air raids were only then beginning in earnest. That spring and summer the nation lived through the trauma of the fall of France, the Dunkirk evacuation, and the Battle of Britain.

Many girls made their way to school in the mornings past buildings which had been bombed and set on fire the previous night. They picked their way round fire hoses and puddles. Because of the air raids school opened at ten o'clock in the morning. Margaret O'Connor remembers a lighter moment: "On one occasion we joined a queue outside a sweet shop where there were actually sweets on sale, and didn't arrive in school until half-past ten. We met Sister Veronica and apologised for being late. 'My dears,' she said, 'you live in Small Heath. You are very brave to come to school at all'. I must say I felt a bit of a heel."

Air raid sirens sounded during the day as well, though most were false alarms. On these occasions the girls were marshalled to walled up sections of the school corridors without windows which served as shelters. Apparently anyone who could entertain their fellow pupils was called on to do so, and any gaps were filled by community singing.

On November 26th, 1940, a second evacuation took place, this time to Whitchurch in Shropshire. Slightly less than a hundred girls went, and about twice that number stayed at Vernon Road. With some specialist staff at each site, it was not possible to teach all subjects to both groups. Some were taught at one centre only, and assignments were set and marked for pupils at the other centre. A close watch on this seems to have been kept by His Majesty's Inspectors, who always pronounced themselves more than satisfied with the arrangements and standards of teaching both at Whitchurch and St. Paul's. This second evacuation went on longer than the first, but at the end of the summer term in 1942, after a questionnaire to parents, it was decided to bring the evacuees and staff back as the danger of bombing was effectively over.

Back at St. Paul's there was plenty of war effort going on. Many older girls became enthusiastic members of the Girls' Training Corps, drilling with military precision under the tutelage of two young Army officers who came to school every Friday afternoon. There was also knitting for the forces and "quantities of gloves, socks, scarves and balaclavas were produced, not to mention the efforts of the valiant Sea Boot Sock section, the wool for which had the most revolting odour," as

Class V at Whitchurch High (evacuated 1941–42).

remembered by Bernadette Loftus (Mrs Parsons). Joyce Harler remembers being very happy at school at this time, except for the disappointment of being unable to play hockey because of the barrage balloons on the field.

For several of the war years girls from the school helped with harvesting and farm work in Warwickshire, living at a camp at Princethorpe, near Barford at the end of August. This was enjoyed especially for the camaraderie that existed between pupils and staff, whereby certain teachers were discovered to be "human and jolly", in contrast to their rather awesome school personae.

A particularly responsible duty was that of fire watching in school, carried out by Sixth Formers; "we spent uneventful nights, sleeping peacefully in the Reception Room, and we were paid for it too!" (Dympna Morby).

Despite all the alarms and excitements, contemporary recollections are full of a sense of how school life carried on, and indeed was deliberately kept as normal as possible. Public examinations were taken and passed; pupil numbers increased so that in September, 1944 the total in the Secondary School stood at 327 (an increase of 51 since 1942); new teachers were appointed while long-serving staff continued their dedicated work. Frequently mentioned among these were Miss Hughes, Miss Smith,

Miss Ryan, Miss Mayes, Mr Meixner, Miss Mongey and Miss Innes. Sadly Miss Bell, who had been at St. Paul's since 1919, died on July 12th, 1942, her resignation on account of ill health having been received just two days previously. New staff appointed during the war included Miss Blackband, Miss Williams, Sister Cecilia Thérèse and Sister Ethelbert (later Sister Josephine). As one former pupil pointed out, the austerity of wartime schooling must have been much harder for the staff than for the pupils. "How I would have hated to write out all the school examinations on the blackboard, while keeping an eye out for cheating! Or to be called back from a well-deserved retirement because of the shortage of teachers." (Margaret O'Connor).

As Dympna Morby recalls, "School life in wartime was full of rich diversity – life had an unpredictable edge of excitement. Most of us seemed to escape unscathed from the pain and horror of the wider world. One memory, though, is still strong, a day filled with the quiet sobbing of a girl who had just learnt that her brother would never return from the war."

In the school journal of 1945 it is recorded that there were two days holiday on May 8th and 9th for Victory, with a further day on the 10th for Ascension Day, thus adding a typically spiritual dimension to the celebrations. By that time, as a result of the 1944 Education Act, another significant development in the school's history had occurred, when the Governors, in April, 1945, agreed to ask for recognition as a Voluntary Aided school under the Local Education Authority. The school was to retain control of its capital expenditure, but funding of staff, books and equipment would come from the LEA. Now the school was no longer St. Paul's High School, but would henceforth be known as St. Paul's Grammar School.

Chapter 5

SCHOOL GOVERNORS
(1908–2008)

The Governing Body of St. Paul's, like the teaching staff, has enjoyed great stability and continuity in its membership, with notably long periods of service, especially by Chairs and Clerks.

In June 1907, a Committee of Management, with the duty of supervising the building process, was elected, with Canon Keating, Bishop of Northampton, in the Chair. The first Annual Meeting of the Governing Body was held in July, 1908.

The first Chairman, who served until his death in 1940, was the Right Reverend Monsignor Wheatley, who was also Chairman of the Governors of St. Paul's Training College from 1919.

Writing in the school magazine of 1938, he mentions the school's debt to the Community of Sisters of St. Paul and declares, "Yours was the first Catholic Grant-earning Secondary School for Girls established in this Diocese, and is the only one in this city, but it is second to none of many others, in its handsome and commodious buildings, full equipment and splendid surroundings."

Monsignor Wheatley was succeeded by Father Vincent Reade of the Birmingham Oratory, a former Headmaster of St. Philip's Grammar School for Boys. He was Chairman from 1940 until 1952.

At that time the majority of the Governing Body would have been clerics, often famous in the Birmingham of their day; such were Father Geoffrey Walmsley, Provost of the Oratorian Fathers, and Canon Eugene O'Sullivan.

From 1952, the first lay Chairman took office; he was Mr Arthur P. Braddock, K.S.G, Head of the Department of Education at the University of Birmingham. Dr.

Gerard Coghlan, K.S.G, who went on to succeed Mr Braddock in 1966, remembers him as "a formidable man – a Knight of St. Gregory" who, he was pleased to discover, had been his father's tutor at training college in Hammersmith.

Dr. Coghlan served as Chairman until 2002, and has seen many changes to the Governing Body since he was appointed to it in 1964, first as a representative of the City Council and then as a Foundation Governor nominated by the Community. He notes that "the Governing Body has been increased several times by statutory legislation, and more recently by the appointment of more Parent Governors. There are also now governors to represent teaching and non-teaching staff. There has been a notable increase in lay strength… certainly in my time very few laymen were on the Governing Body. They were mainly clerical men and ladies."

After 1923 there have always been representatives of the City council on the Governing Body. Notable Councillors remembered by Dr. Coghlan were Sir Francis Griffin, who went on to become Leader of the Council, Mr Lockey, also a very eminent teacher in Birmingham, Councillor Mrs Longden Parker, daughter of a leading Labour politician and Councillor Bill Jarvis, a very famous Socialist and Labour Party member who was a great supporter of the school and a very helpful contact with the Local Education Authority.

Another long-serving Governor from 1968 was Alderman Denis Martineau, who died in 1999. He was Lord Mayor in 1986, following a family tradition, and was another great supporter of the school, and enthusiastic attender at school functions.

Dr. Gerard Coghlan resigned from the post of Chairman in 2002. Having continued for some time to serve as Vice-Chair, he stood down for health reasons, but continues to attend meetings in an advisory capacity, always with a lively interest in and support for the school. He has been succeeded as Chair by Mrs Mary Browning, who previously served both as a Parent and a Foundation Governor.

A relatively recent development has been the inclusion of representatives from the teaching and non-teaching staff on the Governing Body. Among these have been Mrs May, Mrs Brennan, Mr Earp, Mr Ubhi and Miss McCauley.

Just as the Governing Body has had very few Chairs, there has been only a handful of Clerks. At first there were two separate offices of Secretary and Treasurer, the first Secretary, from 1908, being Mr H.R. Hodgkinson, succeeded in 1926 by Mr A.J. Gateley who held office until 1955. The first Treasurer was Alderman T.A. Williams, followed from 1940 by Mr T.F. Holman. In 1955 the offices were merged under the title of Clerk to the Governors and Mr Holman continued in this post until 1969. Mr

Bertie Tuckey then became Clerk and continued his service till 2001, when he was succeeded by Mr W.J. Hunter, who had previously served as a Parent Governor.

Thus the Governing Body has had only five Clerks, or Secretaries, and five Chairs, during a hundred year period which has seen only six Head Teachers. This stability has enabled Governors to support the School through much change, indeed on occasion upheaval, such as the move to comprehensive status in the 1970s. The Governing Body is now larger and more diverse than at any previous time, and has become more closely involved in the management of the school through departmental links and the work of its various Committees, as well as the more informal and social aspects of school life such as entertainments and Awards ceremonies.

Chapter 6

THE POST-WAR GRAMMAR
(1945–1959)

Although the war had ended, the second half of the 1940s saw a period of austerity and "making do" for St. Paul's as well as the nation. Clothing was rationed until 1949 and this made the provision of uniform difficult, especially for those taller or perhaps with larger feet than the average. The latter were measured and weighed in the gym to see if they might be eligible for some extra coupons in addition to the regulation annual 66 for each person.

Gill Methley-Smith (Mrs McKinley) recalled, "In the bitter winter of 1947, girls were allowed to wear any kind of thick sweater as long as it was approximately navy." Another pupil, Juanita Byrne-Quinn, remembered that her jumper "just made the grade, in light blue thick-knit wool in a sort of basket stitch that sat around me like a rug."

Also during that winter Birmingham was plagued by thick fogs, or perhaps more accurately in those pre-Clean Air Act days, smogs. Apparently Sister Gertrude, in the School Office, used to telephone the Corporation Bus Office to get an estimate of how long the buses would continue to run on foggy days. "Mostly she got it right enough for us to get into Colmore Row. Thereafter was more problematical."

Fuel too was in short supply, and when girls arrived cold and wet on winter mornings, they were taken into the Domestic Science Room, Sister Ailbe's domain, to be dried out by the open oven doors. Even in 1952 the food shortages still had their impact on the curriculum, and more particularly on Sister Ailbe's Domestic Science lessons. Doreen Morris (née Bryan) remembers the recipe book compiled during those lessons, containing directions such as: "one tablespoon of sugar, or two if you can afford it," and many lists of ingredients specifying "half an egg". She is still not sure what happened to the other half! Doreen also recalled "carrying a two pound jam jar containing Brown Stew on two buses from Edgbaston to Solihull (but I do not know how much food value remained by the time it reached home)."

In 1948 fees (£4 a term for those not receiving help) were abolished, and each year the numbers taking the entrance examination rose dramatically. By September 1950, the roll numbered 435, rising by 1955 to 629. The school was very small for these growing numbers. In the early 1950s there was still no P.E. changing room. The gym at that time was where the present Canteen now stands, there being from 1948 a purpose built canteen on the site where later the caretaker's house was built. The playing field had a distinct slope towards the reservoir. According to Gill Methley-Smith, "It was a secret delight to watch the faces of the opposing hockey teams when they first visited us to play a match. Often it was a point decidedly in our favour." (The field was eventually levelled in 1961).

At this time the library was housed in what is now a classroom on the top corridor, while the present library was a science laboratory. Some classrooms were extremely small and overcrowded;

Top: Hockey team, c. 1949.
Centre: Form 2J, 1948–49.
Bottom: Tennis team with Miss Williams,
1948–49.

at one stage a room designed to take 30 desks housed 39. Philippa Jordan recalls that there was one modern feature. "Each room was wired to receive school radio broadcasts, with the central control in the Secretary's office. The teacher would set

Hockey team.

the programme there and return to the classroom to find there was no sound or only a squeak. Meanwhile some class elsewhere was receiving details of Hannibal crossing the Alps at full blast! Often half a lesson was wasted in making adjustments. On one occasion I sat for half a programme holding two wires attached to the speaker."

In 1954 the school Log recorded that work had been begun by Messrs. Sapcote on extensions to the school. Three laboratories and two preparation rooms were added at the back of the school, together with a large needlework room on the corridor leading down from the front. This had an Art room above (much later to become a Science laboratory).

In the 1958 Golden Jubilee Magazine, Sheila Gledhill commented that to returning Old Girls, "I doubt if the frontage of St. Paul's would seem very much changed; but they have only to go to the back of the building to see the extensions adjoined to the parts of the school with which they were familiar." This has in fact continued to be true over the second fifty years of the school's life, except for the caretaker's house which appeared on the left-hand side of the building in place of the old Canteen. Considerable additions and alterations have been made at the rear, though in 1966 the main front was extended on the right-hand side, after several years of delays and hitches with plans. This extension added Sixth Form accommodation on the first floor, including a Common Room, a Language Laboratory, an English room and a number of smaller teaching rooms, with classrooms on the ground floor for History, Geography and Modern Languages. The rear part of this new extension made a very big difference to the accommodation, with the spacious New Hall with a proper stage and a large gymnasium at the back. The front extension still stands, but in fact most of it had to be replaced after the disastrous fire of 1974. Unfortunately only one generation of pupils knew the Sixth Form rooms and upstairs Common room, as they were completely destroyed. Now further considerable additions have been made by filling in the upstairs space and extending into the central courtyard. The growth and re-adaptation of the buildings at St. Paul's is a tribute to the ingenuity of successive headmistresses and the support of the Congregation, rarely with huge assistance from local or national government.

In 1966 one of the most welcome additions was the large stage in the New Hall. Sister Josephine (previously Sister Ethelbert) recorded in the school Log that the girls were "delighted to have a proper stage on which to produce their plays." (The House Plays, which for the first time were able to be shown to the whole school together).

Previously any stage production and indeed prize-givings and assemblies had to take place in the original, now the "Old" Hall. A temporary stage was erected there in December each year for

Top: Public examination in the Gym, 1951.
Centre: Science lesson with Miss Jones, 1952.
Bottom: The Library
(now a Form room), 1952.

the Prize-giving Ceremony (very formal with staff in academic dress). Philippa Jordan recalls, "The stage was uncurtained and rather rickety (a display of Irish dancing put a strain on it)." The stage would remain in situ until January for Miss

Heather's annual pantomime, which she produced every year from 1950 to 1955. These were apparently always a great success, and sound extremely ambitious productions especially considering the technical limitations. Miss Heather (nicknamed Heatherbell) had obviously grasped the essential principle of securing a large audience: to have as numerous a cast as possible. "Aladdin" in 1953 involved more than 250 girls, more than half the school at the time. A different whole junior class would take part in each scene, and as Mary Smith (Biology teacher and later Deputy Head) says "all were stars courtesy of Miss Heather."

These were not the only dramas involving St. Paul's pupils. From 1944 there were the joint productions with St. Philip's. These were directed first by Mr Arthur Hunt, who is quoted in Margaret Worsley's *History of St. Philip's* as follows: "We had the complete cooperation of St. Paul's who sent us the loveliest girls you could imagine. They brought a warm civilising influence to Hagley Road." The 1946 production of *Macbeth* seems to have been particularly exciting (and typically jinxed). Peter Wells, who was the Stage Manager, recalls, "It was a very successful production, but not without its moments of panic and terror!

Top: The Canteen, (demolished and replaced by Caretaker's House) 1951.
Centre: The Gym, (now the Canteen) 1951.
Bottom: Craft lesson, 1950s.

On the second night Banquo (Bernard Concannon) was accidentally stabbed in the earlobe and Macbeth (Paul Gudge) after what seemed at the time to be a minor armpit nick sustained during his fight with Macduff, ended up in hospital having gallons of blood removed from his lung. Arthur Hunt could be seen pacing the Hall during the following morning attempting to learn Macbeth's lines – the show must go on!"

Macbeth was followed by *A Midsummer Night's Dream* and *Twelfth Night*. From 1949, Mr Gilchrist became the director, beginning with "The Merchant of Venice". Later, in the 1960s, Mr Peter Dowden took over with some ambitious productions, including one of *Twelfth Night* performed in the grounds of his own house in Worcester in 1962.

These joint productions were virtually all of Shakespeare and are generally agreed to have been of an extremely high standard. They continued until 1972 with John Webster's *The White Devil*, and along with St. Paul's own tradition of House Plays provided enjoyment and excitement which are the "high spot" of many a past pupil's reminiscences.

The House Plays, first mentioned in the School Log in 1959 are remembered by Sue Butler (née Boyle) as, "an important annual event involving much time, commitment and energy in preparation and rehearsal, even before the actual production." The girls themselves were responsible for the whole process which culminated in a drama competition in front of the whole school, judged by Miss Lloyd and the English Department. Then those

Top: Modern Dance in the Old Hall, 1951.
Centre: Craft Class with puppets, 1951–52.
Bottom: Glove puppets, 1951–52.

Co-production with St. Philip's Grammar School – Midsummer Nights Dream, 1947.

plays judged worthy of a public performance were put on for parents. "Choosing the play was the most difficult, as it had to offer a large number of parts and be able to be successfully acted by an all girls' cast… St. Joan's House developed a tradition of productions specialising in lots of chorus speaking by characters of indeterminate gender clad in black tunics and tights – cheap and recyclable!"

These very pupil-centred productions were often most ambitious. Over the years they included *The Importance of Being Earnest, The Trojan Women, Maria Stuart* and *The Lady's Not For Burning*, among many others. Solutions to various staging problems could be ingenious. "The river in *Pilgrim's Progress* involved a rota of first and second years – easily bossed around – hauling yards of black cotton across the stage for what felt like hours on end, while Christian fought Apollyon, got depressed and eventually reached the other side to several rousing verses of *To Be A Pilgrim*."

House Plays continued to be performed usually in October or November until the early 1970s when the house system itself, as in most schools, fell into abeyance. The joint St. Paul's/St. Philip's productions also ceased around this time, with the transformation of St. Philip's from a boys' grammar school into a Sixth Form College.

Co-production with St. Philip's Grammar School – Twelfth Night, 1948.

While describing the links between the two schools, mention must also be made of the joint Literary and Debating Society which flourished from about 1953 until 1973. By the later 1950s there were meetings once a fortnight held alternately at St. Paul's and St. Philip's, led by Mr Dowden and Miss Maureen Shaw. Miss Shaw remembers that topics included nuclear disarmament, apartheid, the emerging women's liberation movement and comprehensive education. But one debate she particularly recalls was in the 1960s when the motion before the House was "This House detests the Beatles and all they stand for" – deliberately set by the committee to be provocative. "The old library at St. Philip's was packed to the rafters and emotions were soon running high. To be honest, I don't recall the actual points made, but the exciting heady atmosphere was something that made a vivid and lasting impression on me. At the end the motion was overwhelmingly defeated, and great was the rejoicing among the multitude of fans."

Passion was still a feature when one of the last debates was held in 1972, again on the subject of female equality, recalled in the St. Philip's magazine, *Pietas*. "The two opening speeches were full of impassioned vehemence... the excellent chairwoman, Margaret Maloney, aided by her minions in the House, managed to convert a 14–15 defeat into a 16–15 victory for St. Paul's by counting the votes of two already departed females. The process was so rapidly accomplished that the St. Philip's contingent were shocked into amazed silence, during which Miss Shaw was heard to mutter something about the superiority of women being exemplified by the sudden reverse they had so skilfully engineered against the boys."

The links between the two schools were hardly surprising in view of the fact that so many girls had brothers at St. Philip's. However, as Juanita Byrne-Quinn comments, "Only the most advanced girls took part in the practice of meeting the boys at The Ivy Bush on a mostly cold, windy and inhospitable corner." There were permitted contacts, though, in the Friday night "hops" held at St. Philip's in the late 1940s and early 50s. Mrs Sheila Downes (née Baikie) who taught Chemistry remembers chaperoning senior girls to dancing classes held jointly with the boys in preparation for these events. They were presided over by the formidable Headmaster at the time, Mr T.J. Larkin. At the Christmas dance Sheila Downes recalls that the staff spent all their time searching for courting couples in various hiding places.

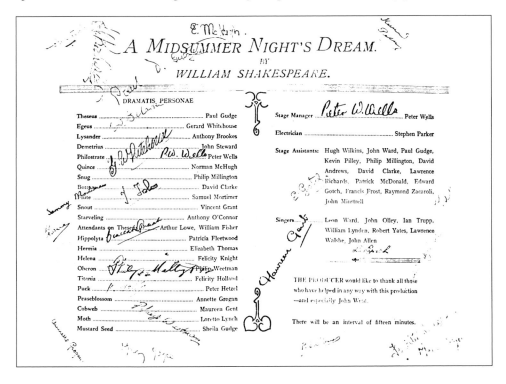

Programme for Midsummer Nights Dream, 1947.

Joint production with St. Philip's Grammar School – Much Ado About Nothing, 1952.

All these contacts did of course lead to romance and marriage, news of which was apparently followed with great interest by Sister Veronica herself. In February, 1948 she recorded with approval in the school Log that a dance organised at the Botanical Gardens by St. Paul's and St. Philip's Old Pupils was a great success, and that tickets had proved inadequate for the demand.

Like Sister Veronica a number of the staff had been there since the 1920s and indeed earlier. The post-war period saw the retirement or departure of some of the longest serving and best remembered of these.

Miss Smith, who had taught Art since the early days, part-time at St. Paul's and part at St. Philip's retired during the latter part of the war, and was replaced by Miss Blackband, herself to become a long-serving teacher. 1949 saw the retirement of Mr Meixner, who had been teaching Maths at St. Paul's since 1912, and had been particularly active in founding and encouraging the Old Girls' Association.

One very sad event of 1949 was the death of Miss Hughes, who had taught Geography since 1921. Apparently the gas heater in her bedroom had developed a leak overnight, and she died in her sleep of gas poisoning. Miss Hughes was remembered as a very effective and thorough Geography teacher, with a habit of springing unforeseen tests, but also for lighter-hearted geography quizzes. In Dympna Morby's recollection she was "a great teacher and personality, indefatigable in giving her time to our out of class activities and never losing her temper – but how we revelled in her turn of phrase as she would wither us with words!"

1953 saw the retirement of the two long serving French teachers, Miss Mongey (remembered as "a temperamental lady of Irish birth, clutching her fur coat around her and talking French at a mile a minute") and Miss Innes, who had been at the school since 1913 and is one of the most often mentioned teachers when Old Girls meet. Miss Jones who had taught Biology for 30 years (St. Paul's having been one of the pioneer schools to introduce the subject) retired in 1954.

There continued at this period to be some real "characters" on the Staff. Sister Gertrude, the Bursar, was described as "scary on the surface but kind hearted and with a wonderfully dry sense of humour underneath." No history of the school would be complete without mention of the unforgettable Sister Cecilia Thérèse, second mistress and Maths teacher. She is remembered by Margaret Beadlin, who taught in the Maths Department at the same time, as "a great character and very good, particularly with the less able." However she could have a ferocious temper at

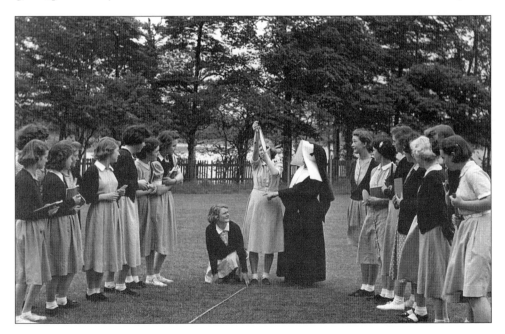

Trigonometry al fresco, 1951–52.

times, and when told of the effect this had on some pupils, retorted, "A little healthy respect never did anyone any harm!"

She was an enthusiastic proponent of the school's link with its adopted ship, H.M.S. Birmingham. Since 1938 the girls had collected newspapers and Catholic periodicals to send to the ship, and had offered prayers for its safety. Many of the sailors were Goanese, and Sister "C.T." could sometimes be diverted from Maths to chatting about them and the ship's progress. Juanita Byrne-Quinn remembers the school visit to the ship in Portsmouth dock in 1950, with a party of 32 girls and 2 Sisters. Apart from "lots of sailors, steel and staircases" her most vivid memory is of "being given cups of hot Bovril to drink and C.T. refusing to let us accept as it was Friday. Even at that time we reckoned that 'on board ship' was a dispensation... But I expect C.T. felt it her duty to keep us very strictly in line."

Margaret Robinson (née Hampson) also remembers Sister Cecilia Thérèse's enthusiasm for H.M.S. Birmingham.

"She would walk around the classroom asking us to empty our purses, and if she spotted a Ship Halfpenny she pocketed it for her cause. I was allocated the task of writing about the school's involvement with the ship for the *Apostleship of the Sea* magazine, and as a reward I and some other girls were taken by Sister for an afternoon out at the Botanical Gardens, a fair walk from school. Once we set off to return the heavens opened and down came a typical summer storm. Did we run for shelter? No. Sister always had an answer for everything. She lifted up her habit and innumerable underskirts and ordered us underneath."

Miss Winifred Mayes spent her last day in school on July 25th, 1961. At that time she was Senior Mistress, Choir Mistress and Upper VI Form mistress, and is still remembered by staff and pupils of the era as 'a linchpin of the school community'. She had come to St. Paul's as a pupil in 1911, and returned to the Staff in 1923. Miss Mayes had taught Music ever since, and was indelibly associated with the choir, taking over its charge from Father Robert in 1925. Many Old Girls still remember the anthems they sang to accompany Benediction, perhaps particularly the "Ave Verum", with near the end, "its devastatingly long note for the nervous sopranos conscious that Miss Mayes's eye was riveted on them to check that they did not draw a breath in the middle of it." (Gill McKinley). Yet she was clearly not one of those teachers with time only for those with musical talent: Jenny Mason (Mrs Bowditch) remembers that "Miss Mayes was so tolerant of my complete lack of singing ability, but encouraged me enough, so that later on in school I helped Barbara Hartland run the Classical Music Society."

Along with the departures there were many arrivals during the post-war period of staff who themselves became longstanding and well-remembered, among them Miss Lloyd, Mrs Samuel, Miss Jordan, Miss Shaw, Miss Mary Smith, Misses Monica and Kathleen Hermolle, Miss Clarkson, Miss Steward, Sister Catherine Murphy (then Sister Baptist) and Sister Hilary Beater (then Sr. Philomene).

From the mid-fifties Mrs Dorothy Hogg was in charge of Modern Languages. She led a number of trips abroad, notably to Brittany. Mary Holland remembers her as "a brilliant organiser, so the holiday was packed with interest; we watched the parade of Breton costumes through the streets of Quimper during the Fête de Cornouailles, visited the Henriot porcelain factory, swam in the sea in the rain, gazed at the carvings in the Calvaries for which Brittany is renowned and climbed up to the Abbey on the top of Mont St. Michel." Indeed trips and excursions seemed to occur frequently in the 1950s and 60s, perhaps when there was less regulation and fear of litigation. Between July 5th and July 14th in 1955, for instance, the log records that Year II went to Chedworth and the Cotswolds, Year III to Warwick castle, the IVs to Shakespeare Country, Year V to Stoneleigh Abbey and the Senior outing was to Oxford and Blenheim.

In October, 1958 the school celebrated its Golden Jubilee. All forms had tea parties, the pupils went to Mass at the Oratory and there was a Pontifical Mass, celebrated by Archbishop Grimshaw, in the Chapel for Old Girls, followed by a Dinner in the Old (and still only) Hall. As Miss Lloyd noted in the School Magazine, "The names of certain giants of the past constantly recurred, notably those of Father Robert and Mr Meixner. All the speeches were full of happy reminiscences of the past and confident hopes for the future."

At the end of the following term, in March, 1959, Sister Veronica Marie Groves retired after thirty-six years of devoted service. The girls presented her with a cheque, and with typical care for the school she directed it should be used for the purchase of a grand piano. Sister Veronica had guided the school through a period of tremendous change and development, while maintaining and enhancing its strong traditions. She was remembered as "a sweet, gentle head", who allowed staff who travelled home some distance at weekends to come in late on Monday mornings rather than travel back on Sunday night.

Hon. Alderman Mrs Marian Arnott-Job (née Frain, who in 1996 served as Lord Mayor of Birmingham) recalled Sister Veronica's particular kindness to her when she and her family came to the city from Ireland immediately after the war. "The move from the convent school in Ireland, where all the lessons were taught in Gaelic was

Sister Veronica retires, 1958.

indeed a traumatic one, but I was warmly welcomed and settled in quickly… I enjoyed my time at the school immensely."

Nevertheless she was also a figure of considerable authority. When some of the Upper V had the temerity to go "on strike" during a French lesson it was Sister Veronica who "quelled that rebellion by having us into her room, one by one, looking down her nose at us, and remarking on our lack of ladylikeness and general unworthiness as members of St. Paul's."

Her standards were high: she could often be seen at the end of school checking the girls' hats and gloves as they went out of the door. Any girl reported as eating ice cream on the street was treated as a sinner. There was a sense of quiet awe about her as a disciplinarian, however; she was said to move through the school almost silently, save for the faint rattling of her rosary beads. Society as well as the school had moved on almost out of recognition since Sister Veronica had become Headmistress in 1923, and the next decade was to present further turbulence and challenge for her successor.

Chapter 7

SCHOOL UNIFORM

Wherever groups of old school friends meet, at any rate in the United Kingdom, the talk and reminiscing inevitably turns to the old school uniform, and often to the particular ways found by the wearers in each generation of customising it to put their own stamp on what the authorities intended to be a regulation costume.

The earliest St. Paul's prospectus gives few specific details about uniform apart from requiring that "each girl must be provided with a pair of shoes for Schoolroom wear, a pair of tennis shoes and a navy blue costume for drill." We know that on special occasions such as the Opening Ceremony, and Prize Givings, girls were dressed in white (a custom which continued into the 1930s for the Choir, and also for processions and certain feast days).

Agnes Deeley, who attended school from 1912 to 1918, remembered wearing "white blouses and blue tunics in summer, with red blouses and blue tunics in winter. We had to tie our hair back with a navy ribbon. For those who hadn't got a ribbon, Miss Innes supplied one. She gave one to me and I wouldn't wear it. I gave it back and for my insurrection I nearly got expelled."

Evelyn Newbery (1918–1924) recalled, "We wore a panama hat in the summer and a blazer, and in winter we had navy coats and felt hats, scarves and woolly gloves. Our gym slips were to be worn just below the knee, and to make sure we were quite respectable we were tested individually by one of the sisters by kneeling down so that the bottom of the gymslip touched the floor." Theresa Gay (Mrs Priest) also attended St. Paul's from 1918. She too recalls the tunics "with three box-pleats back and front, a braid girdle knotted at the waist, worn with a white blouse and the school tie. The same costume was worn for P.E., but with pumps."

Skirt length was as much of an obsession for the wearers and the enforcers as it has been throughout British schoolgirl history. According to Cora Davies (Mrs Jacobs), a pupil from 1926, and therefore the "Flapper" era, "We were not supposed to wear short skirts, but we used to pull our tunics up over our girdles, so that they sort of bloused out, and then pulled the skirt well above our knees, till we were caught by somebody, who'd say, 'Change that at once, girl!'" She also recollects that they could not go out into the street without a hat – felt in winter, straw in summer. By this stage a tie had been introduced, in the school colours of navy, white and yellow stripes, and blazers with the school badge were worn. Cora also remembered the thick black stockings; "We were always pulling at them to keep them up, so we had holes in our stockings! Horrible things!"

Eileen Shaw (née Hemus) can remember the tunic, black stockings and panama hats from the list she was given after passing the 11–plus in 1934. There was a summer dress, worn with lisle stockings, though she remembers many girls taking a pair of socks to come home in. (Woe betide anyone caught thus attired by the nuns!) "We had black pumps to wear in school and white ones for P.E. and Games. When it was found that some girls were borrowing pumps for Games, we had to sew our initials in white on our black pumps, and in black on our white ones. We then had to stand in a line for each lesson while the P.E. mistress walked along looking at us and our pumps!"

The requirement for a pair of indoor shoes for school wear carried on at least until the 1950s. No doubt this protected the highly polished floors recalled by a number of pupils. Changing shoes could be a chore. "Sister Annunciata's injunctions to me to 'Hurry up, Theresa Gay' did not assist my nervous fingers as I tried to loosen the cross lacings on my knee high boots after the mile long walk back from home at lunch time."

Although the War and the exigencies of rationing, together with the fact pupils were no longer fee-paying, loosened the regulations to some degree, uniform continued to be both strictly upheld by authority and at the same time subverted by its wearers. Joan McHale, a pupil in the 1950s, describes the uniform of that era: "the striped tie, the purse on a cord worn diagonally across the body, the panama hat with elastic under the chin, and then the beret, which as we got older we rarely wore in the correct fashion, but flat on the back of the head and held in place by grips… we obviously thought it more attractive that way. There was a blue summer dress; the skirt was quite full as it was gathered onto the bodice." The "panama" referred to seems to have been superseded by the boater which Philippa Jordan remembers as having been proposed by the School Council, for wear by Third Year upwards. "These may have been stylish, but were not particularly comfortable, especially when tipped over the wearer's eyes by the St. Philip's boys on the bus."

In the early 1950s winter hats were of velour with hat bands. These were unpopular but it was not until the 1960s that Sr. Josephine introduced a small navy felt model, with the school badge on. These had a shallow upturned brim and a short ribbon hanging jauntily at the back. The School Log for 1965 records a concession that girls taking part in Saturday matches need no longer wear their hats. With the Sixties in full swing they must have been very relieved.

Some girls attempted to widen further the already full-skirted summer dresses by adopting the 50s fashion for many layered underskirts (impractical for getting through doors!) The Sixth Form, who at this time also wore uniform, were allowed to choose their own material: Miss Jordan remembers a dark navy, and a blue and gold stripe on a white ground. In 1966 the Sixth Form were granted the option of not wearing school uniform on Fridays (an early forerunner of "dress-down Fridays!"), but it was not until the 1970s that they were able to abandon uniform, and fight a successful battle to be allowed to wear trousers, at least two years before a similar option was available to staff. In 1974 a daring teacher went to ask the fairly newly-appointed Sister Agnes whether she would object to staff (i.e. the female ones) wearing trousers. The answer was favourable, and Mrs Samuel, who happened to have a pair with her for some after school occasion, went and got changed immediately.

Sixth form dress was supposed to be "suitable for office wear", till the great day in September, 1990 when Sister Thérèse (the result of another plea to a newly-appointed Head!) announced that jeans could be worn.

There had been a P.E. uniform of some kind since the 1920s; in the 1950s divided skirts were worn, and these too were the subject of regulation. Doreen Bryan (Mrs Morris) remembers "being asked, while in the queue waiting to enter the gym, whether perhaps my mother could stitch a frill onto my divided skirt to lengthen it. I had obviously grown taller and the shorts were now more than the regulation two inches from the ground when I was kneeling."

As time went on the summer dresses were gradually abandoned; by the 1970s fewer parents were used to home dressmaking, and a separate uniform for one term which often began anyway with a cool spell was seen as impractical. Blazers also for many schools became a less familiar part of uniform and St. Paul's was no exception. The focus for battles over uniform came to centre on shoes and skirts. As with most institutions, it was easy to ban stiletto heels on grounds of the awful damage to floors;

platform soles and heels were more of a danger to the wearers' ankles but appeared from time to time according to the dictates of fashion. Helen Peters (née Stewart) remembers tripping over in the Old Hall and spraining her ankle when wearing high brown platform shoes. These went with the brown uniform which her particular Sixth Form had designed for themselves in 1974.

Apart from the aforementioned fashion for wide skirts and a period in the early 70s when skirts became too "maxi" for the regulations, the miniskirt has continued as much a bone of contention as it was in the 20s, though now usually achieved by rolling over several inches of material at the waistband. All who attended school in Sr. Agnes's reign will remember how the "four-gore skirt" became one of her catchphrases, to be lovingly recalled in various sketches especially at the time of her retirement.

So the wheel of fashion turns; the latest smart addition to St. Paul's uniform is the tracksuit worn for P.E. and much approved by the present generation of schoolgirls.

Throughout at least the last 25 years suggestions have come from form and School Council meetings that trousers should become part of the everyday uniform. So far, the school has resisted this development, but who knows what changes a future historian will have to record? The one certainty is that the uniform will continue to be a lively bone of contention for those who wear it, and a source of nostalgia and reminiscence wherever Old Girls meet.

ST. PAUL'S HIGH SCHOOL,
VERNON ROAD,
EDGBASTON

SCHOOL OUTFIT.

INDOOR.

1.—Navy Blue Drill Tunic (made with three box-pleats back and front). Girdle of navy blue braid.
2.—Navy knickers.
3.—Blouses—white, with long sleeves gathered into a cuff at the wrists.
4.—Indoor shoes and a bag to keep them in.
5.—An extra pair of stockings to be kept in school.
6.—Rubber pumps for gymnastics.

OUTDOOR.

1.—A black or navy felt hat for winter wear and a white or cream straw for summer, with a ribbon band of the school colours. The hats should be plain in shape.
2.—A navy coat.
N.B.—No jewellery is to be worn in school.

THE TUNIC.

A good hem should be turned up at the bottom of the tunic, and the straps should lap over where they button on the shoulder, so that the tunic can be lengthened as required.
The length should be 3 ins. from the ground when measured from a kneeling position

ST. PAUL'S HIGH SCHOOL, VERNON ROAD, EDGBASTON
'Phone: EDGbaston 0606 1707

SCHOOL OUTFIT.

INDOOR.

1.—A navy pinafore dress with gored skirt and a neck V shaped in front, fastening on shoulders with buttons (to allow for lengthening), Pocket in the side. Navy belt of material. (Illustration enclosed).
2.—Navy shorts for gymnastics (divided skirts with box pleats as shown in illustration).
3.—White blouses, with long sleeves and turn over collars. Worn with tie.
4.—Indoor shoes and rubber pumps.
5.—White ankle socks or fawn stockings.
6.—Navy blazer. Optional, but very useful.

SUMMER TERM.

A dress of pale blue rayon material. (Can be procured at school if desired). White or cream hat.

OUTDOOR.

1.—Navy hat, with School band and badge.
2.—Navy coat.
N.B.—No jewellery is to be worn in school. Hat bands and badges are procurable in School.

School uniform list.

50

Chapter 8

CHALLENGES AND CHANGE
(1959–1974)

In April, 1959 Sister Ethelbert took over as Headmistress. She had taught at St. Paul's since 1944, and had latterly been Head of English. She was a lady with several names as well as many talents. Following a sabbatical in the 1950s to complete a Ph.D in mediaeval literature at Birmingham University, she was addressed as Dr. Cooper on most official correspondence. In the later 1960s, following the Congregation's decision that Sisters might henceforth be known by their own baptismal names, rather than that of a chosen saint, Sister Ethelbert became Sister Josephine.

Dr. Gerard Coghlan, for many years Chairman of Governors, still delights to tell how his son as a small boy took a telephone call from the Headmistress, and shouted through to his father that Engelbert Humperdinck wanted a word with him! When she called at the house that weekend he introduced himself to her. She gravely replied, "And I am Sister Engelbert," at which, his father records, "He went pinker than I have ever seen anyone go."

Mary Cusack (Mrs Levesley) remembers Sister Josephine with gratitude from English lessons in the 1950s. "I learned how to read with intelligent enjoyment." Sister told her class of how, when she was about to enter the novitiate, she was informed that her religious name would be Ethelbert. "She was shocked, and said, 'I've never heard of Ethelbert!'

'Well, you will be hearing it a lot from now on,' was the reply. I can't say I was surprised when I heard that when nuns were allowed to keep their own names she reverted to Josephine."

It fell to Sister Josephine to lead the school through a particularly sticky patch in its history. This arose chiefly from two sets of circumstances. One was that while the school was expanding in numbers accommodation was becoming more cramped and in need of repair. This was an ongoing saga which appeared to have reached a satisfactory conclusion in 1966 with the opening of the new extension on the front with Sixth form rooms, but suffered a savage twist with the fire of 1973, just towards the end of Sr. Josephine's headship.

The other challenge was presented by the national movement towards non-selective education, and consequently the various schemes for reorganisation presented by the LEA and the diocese. Reorganisation became a perpetual source of controversy and heart searching which was not finally resolved until 1975.

The main history of the alterations to the School buildings has been covered in a previous chapter but it is worth noting again the time spent and anxiety caused between 1961 and 1966 by the various objections to and refusals of planning permission, and consequent alterations to plans, against a background of a growing school roll. The Sixth Form, for instance, numbered 74 in 1963, had increased to 100 by 1967, 118 in 1969 and stood at 127 in 1972.

Mrs Downes and Chemistry class, 1960s.

Top left: Miss Pat Dougherty and class, early 1960s. Bottom left: Tennis Team, 1951.
Right: Mrs Meyrick and Miss Shaw dressed for tennis.

Some of the pressure was eased by the closure of the Preparatory School in 1962. The Convent classrooms thus vacated were offered to the school as temporary accommodation until the new extensions were complete. These rooms are still in use today, with a vastly increased amount of the Convent being given over to school use.

It was a particularly difficult struggle to get planning permission for a caretaker's house on the School site. This was twice refused but eventually the house was completed in 1968, built on the site of the old Canteen. Nor would the LEA provide the funding for new tennis courts to replace those which had been swallowed up by the new hall and gymnasium. A fund-raising committee was formed by Sr. Josephine, and eventually replacement courts were created at the rear of the new building.

As far as the pupils were concerned school went on much as usual. Jenny Bowditch (née Mason) recalls the 1960s with great affection. She remembers battered Spam and chocolate concrete in the Canteen, Miss Smith riding her bicycle down Hagley Road, Sister Gertrude in the office, "always lovely to me", and the staff versus pupils hockey matches. Some of her most vivid memories are of Sr. Josephine's

53

assemblies. It seemed as though every morning Sister was "shocked and distressed to learn" of some new transgression by the pupils, such as the day when some greedy girl asked for seconds at dinner time and when refused had called the lady in the canteen "a skinny cat". There was a special afternoon assembly that day so that the girl could own up by 4p.m.!

Her other abiding memory of St. Paul's is of her last day when some of the Upper VI replaced the chairs in the staff room with gym equipment. The whole form had to spend the final assembly carrying all the equipment back, having caused considerable "shock and distress." They forfeited the usual token of a holy picture on their school leaving. Nevertheless she concludes, "It was a very special school and I am so grateful to have had a place there."

Holy pictures are also alive in the memory of Margaret Sutherland (née Sharkey), from the later 1960s (Margaret has been a very successful teacher of Maths for many years now at St. Paul's). Sister Virgil (to become Sr. Margaret) was her form teacher in 2Y. She taught them R.E. and anyone who stuck a holy picture in their R.E. homework was sure of an A. She also remembers Sr. Josephine taking each first year class once a week for a poetry lesson; they seemed to spend a long time on Hiawatha.

Sister Ailbe, (Home Economics) c. 1960.

Left: Mrs Millington and Rosemary Bell, 1961. Top right: Upper VI, 1965.
Bottom right: Botany Trip, 1965.

Sport continued to provide a great deal of enjoyment. Margaret McGuire (née O'Loughlin) played netball and rounders for the school from 1956 to 1963 and has "happy memories of doing battle in far flung areas of Birmingham… always dreading of course the role of 'cancellation number' for any given Saturday… having to be up early to do battle with the telephone lines."

Back at school she remembers being kept on track by "order marks and detentions plus the swish of skirts and the rattle of beads from various hidden corners." One of her classmates spent "hours it seems standing beneath a statue in the Hall – supposedly praying for guidance after her many misdemeanours. As she was also the 3A culprit who changed a blackboard heading written by Sister Baptist 'How to plan a menu for a family of four' by erasing the words 'a menu', I'm not really surprised."

Sister Baptist will be remembered by many more girls as Sister Catherine, Head of Home Economics for many years and a really strong pillar of the school community. School events were always enhanced, not only by her catering but by her

Mrs Benbow and Gym class, early 1960s.

organisational flair. Things could go wrong on occasion, though. Caroline Rathmell (née Neary) remembers an occasion from around 1970 when Sister Catherine asked her class to make mince pies for their Parents' Evening.

"Sister Catherine asked me to collect a large clear glass jar (one of three similar, and all unlabelled) from a high shelf. I picked up the one I thought she had indicated and brought it back to the table to sieve the icing sugar over the trays of mince pies. I remember thinking that it sieved easily. When we had finished Sister came over and detected that I had selected salt instead of icing sugar, and was obviously not impressed! We were then ordered to dust off as much of the salt as we could and smother the pies in icing sugar.

"I hardly slept that night and warned my mother not to eat a mince pie at the Parents' Evening! The following day, Sister Catherine was relieved to tell me that only one parent had commented that the mince pies tasted rather salty!"

In 1959 Miss Monica Hermolle arrived as Physical Education teacher, expecting to feel very strange as an 'Old Girl' on the staff, but she says, in reality made to feel most welcome. Facilities were not so inspiring: "the old gym was very small and

Old gym (now Canteen), early 1960s.

sometimes unusable in rainy weather because of the leaks in the flat roof. The field was being levelled and we were left with two good netball/tennis courts and an old hard court. The girls' changing room was a former washroom… however there was great enthusiasm for P.E.…. every Saturday at least one hundred girls played in hockey and netball matches, one in every six girls in school."

There were also very popular dance and gym clubs. Dancers regularly performed for the P.G.C.E. students at Birmingham University. Often they added their own vocal accompaniment as a result of working in 'the hut' without electricity for a term while the old gym was being changed into a dining hall.

The school staff in general were very supportive and there were Staff/Sixth Form matches in various sports. Miss Hermolle says that the most memorable occasions were the staff events for the swimming galas. She recalls particularly the time "when Miss Lloyd dressed as a nun and glided across the water on her back with her arms folded across her chest. The costume had been ingeniously created from crepe paper. As she floated along, the dye radiated out from her outfit and coloured the whole pool an inky blue. The audience erupted with laughter, all except the manager of the

Sister Cecilia Thérèse.

swimming bath." Apparently next day the pool had to be drained and the water entirely refilled.

Amidst all the fun and activity, several sad events are noted in the School Log for this period. In April, 1964, a promising student and keen sportswoman, Maureen Murphy, died following a car accident while on holiday with her friend Jennifer Pozzi in Scotland.

Just before Christmas in 1966 Susan Greatorex of 2Z was walking the last few yards of her journey home after attending a House party for First and Second Year pupils. She was knocked down by a car and killed. Sr. Josephine always later remembered attending her funeral on a dank and chilly Christmas Eve. In May, 1969, a First Year pupil, Lorna Harris, sadly died of leukaemia.

But of course there were happier days and celebrations. On October 11th, 1968 the Old Girls met to celebrate the School's Diamond Jubilee, and Sister Veronica's Golden Jubilee. Over 300 attended, including four Old Girls who had been present at the Opening Day in 1908.

On a number of occasions St. Paul's had a celebrity visitor. Ruth Hayes (née Fulford) remembers one of them.

Sister Catherine Murphy.

"One of the highlights of my days at St. Paul's was the visit of Dame Sybil Thorndike in 1969 when I was in second year. I knew she was a famous actress who had performed the definitive St. Joan in Shaw's play. St. Joan was one of my dad's favourite plays and my oldest sister was called Helen Joan in homage. I was thrilled to be seeing this lady in the flesh, coming apparently at Mrs Hogg's invitation. Fond as I was of Mrs Hogg, who was a good-natured, kind lady, I couldn't see a connection between her and film stars. She was a Quaker and plain-speaking and full of common sense.

"I had another surprise when Dame Sybil walked on to the stage in the New Hall to speak to the assembled school, for she turned out to be a little old lady with white hair, slightly bent. She was in fact 87 years old. But when she spoke her voice was strong and clear.

"She didn't tell us about her illustrious career as a famous actress. She told us about a more important mission. She was passionate in her pursuit of peace and justice for all, and her resonant words were inspirational. We left the assembly glowing.

"I've found out since that in that same year Dame Sybil spoke at a meeting in London to observe the centenary of Gandhi's birth. I wonder if she travelled from St.

Paul's to that meeting, or perhaps came from speaking to that huge assembly of followers of Gandhi to speak at St. Paul's, to an assembly of young women just starting out in life."

The 1960s was a decade of considerable upheaval and change in education. The minutes of the Governors' meeting of March, 1965 record that Father Emery, Head of the Birmingham Diocesan Schools Commission had asked for the governors' views on reorganisation, in view of the plans being discussed by the LEA for its secondary schools. He had apparently sent a verbal message (!) to the Head asking what the reaction would be to the idea of St. Paul's becoming a mixed Sixth Form College. Mother Maria Pia (the Congregation's mistress in charge of schools) was present, and pointed out that according to the articles of government a member of the Community should be in charge of the school, whereas a mixed college would probably require a Headmaster. (Whatever we may now think of this, it suggests quick thinking on her part!)

During the latter part of the decade most city secondary schools were reorganised, and various suggestions were made as to how the Catholic and the voluntary aided sector might comply with Government policy. In September, 1972, Father Reilly presented a plan for the reorganisation of Catholic secondary schools in Birmingham. St. Paul's would become a 5–form entry 13–18 girls' non-selective school, part of a consortium consisting of St. Philip's, St. Paul's, St. Michael's and St. Chad's.

There was strong opposition from parents and from the staff of both St. Paul's and St. Philip's. At a parents' meeting to discuss the plan there was an attendance of over 600. In October the Governors decided formally that they were unable to accept the scheme as it affected St. Paul's. For a time St. Paul's and the other Catholic and non-Catholic voluntary aided schools were in a difficult position. As a group they gave notice that they could not accept the date of September 1973 for any reorganisation. Nevertheless St. Paul's governors clearly stated they were willing to discuss any new plans. Many will remember that at this time Councillor Sheila Wright was the Chair of the Education Committee, and there were a number of meetings between her, Chief Education Officer Brooksbank and the various Heads and governors. There was difficulty with selection procedures as the eight dissenting schools were not included in the booklet sent out by the LEA to junior schools to inform parental choice.

One particular problem for St. Paul's was the way the city was to be divided up into catchment areas; St. Paul's had previously had very little geographical restriction on its intake, and the catchment area at first proposed was very much based on the inner city area and therefore unlikely to provide a real mixed ability spread. At one meeting with the authorities in March, 1974, Reverend Mother Malachy Joseph stipulated that if St. Paul's went into the scheme then under discussion they should have a wider catchment area, and they should remain an all girls 11–18 school. By this time the school was coping with the after effects of the fire of 1974, and she felt justified in asking for it to be treated as a special case, due to the damage and the lack of accommodation for practical subjects. After another meeting the governors were offered two other sites for a future St. Paul's building, but nothing further came of this. In June, 1974 the governing body agreed to approve in principle "the working towards re-organisation of the School on non-selective lines."

In December of that year, a further resolution was passed "that henceforth the character of St. Paul's Grammar School be changed in so far that girls will be admitted without reference to ability or aptitude." Accordingly in September, 1975 St. Paul's received its first comprehensive intake of 122 girls (the total number on roll at the time being 603). Dr. Gerard Coghlan comments, "Our big success was to have for our catchment area the whole of the city. Thus we didn't become comprehensive in the sense it was used at the time, because then we would only have had a wedge of the city, and we felt we owed a duty right from our foundation to the people and girls of all the city."

Top: Front extension rebuilt after fire, 1978–79.
Bottom: Report of fire in 1974
(from Evening Mail).

A year earlier Sister Josephine had retired. She had faced arguably the greatest challenges to the school in the problems with buildings and the biggest change in the nature of the school in its history. She combined a deceptively gentle manner with a steely determination to do the best for the school, and an intellectual rigour, a combination fondly remembered by her pupils, especially those whom she taught in her days as Head of English. They remember the liveliness of her teaching, especially at A-level, as well as the copious amounts of homework (and she was always able to keep up with the marking!) It is frequently remarked by staff and pupils from her time that she was a lady in the true sense of that word.

The other unforeseen challenge she had to face, which, together with poor health probably precipitated her retirement, was the fire of November, 1974. Margaret Czepiel, then a Year 8 pupil and now Head of R.E.

Top: The Staff, 1973.
Bottom: Miss Lloyd and Sixth Form
English group, 1960s.

remembers coming down Vernon Road and seeing a wisp of smoke rising up behind some trees. "Wouldn't it be funny," she thought, "if school burnt down?" It had, and as she recalls, it wasn't funny at all. The painters decorating the older part of the building had a hut in the open space between the New Hall and the Geography Room. Here they left a heater on so that the temperature of the paint stayed constant. In fact the paint heated up enough to cause an explosion and subsequent fire. Virtually all the lovely new Sixth Form block with its common room, language laboratory and study rooms as well as classrooms had gone. Even the rooms in the old Upper Corridor leading into the new block smelt of smoke for years, as did whole sets of books rescued from waterlogged stock cupboards.

Miss Czepiel remembers the "calming solemn influence of Sister Josephine as the pupils squeezed into the Old Hall, said a prayer and made arrangements to go home." Yet very little school time was missed, though the consequent rebuilding caused disruption for a long time. The convent classrooms which had belonged to the preparatory school came into service again, and prefabricated classrooms were erected at the rear of the convent, where they remained until 2007, though long past their sell-by date. The rooms in the convent eventually became the headquarters of the much expanded Business Studies and Information Technology departments. A final memory of Sister Josephine comes from Margaret O'Brien (née Bryan), another former pupil who became Head of Business Studies in the 1980s.

"Several times a week I would meet Sister Josephine. She was my form teacher during Lower Fifth and also taught me English. She was always pleased to stop and chat about the 'old days'. She was spending her retirement at Vernon Road with small groups of Sixth Form students, helping with their A-level studies – they were very lucky girls!"

Top: 3H, Sr. Hilary and Mrs Hopkins, 1971. Bottom: Sr. Josephine, Mrs Siekierski, Mrs Agnes Lambert, early 1970s.

Chapter 9

SCHOOL LIFE AND LITURGY

No history of St. Paul's would be complete without a reflection on the liturgical life of the school, from the Year 7 Mass in October which formally welcomes pupils and parents at the beginning of the school career to the Leavers' masses where emotions seesaw between laughter and tears.

Claire Eastwood, Head of R.E. from 1974 till 2006 writes:

"In St. Paul's Masses all that is best in the school is brought together and offered in strands of artistry, creativity, literature, music, drama and dance, with pupil and staff participation; a sensitivity which embraces and entwines our inner and outer reality, the spiritual and the physical, the solitary and the shared.

"Ritual makes time for reflection, reverence and respect, and over the years, be it in the Convent Chapel, the assembly Hall, humble classrooms or on the playing field, it beckons: 'Be silent; Be still'. It has long been the custom in St. Paul's to pray the Angelus at midday, and the community is summoned to stillness and calm by a striking gong."

This is certainly a custom which has been celebrated by generations of pupils, and always impresses visitors, once they have got over the surprise of walking along a corridor at midday and seeing everyone suddenly stop stock still as if in a game of statues. The Angelus bell is still sounded in the Old Hall close to the statue of Our Lady. In the Golden Jubilee magazine of 1958 there is an account by Margaret McGillycuddy of the dedication of the first such statue.

"I think it was for the December 8th, 1908 that we pupils purchased the beautiful statue of Our Lady, and after the unveiling we sang 'This is the image of Our Queen…' I believe it was in June, 1909 that we collected for the statue of the Sacred Heart. The unveiling was a lovely ceremony and we sang 'Sweet Heart of Jesus'."

Another memorable tradition is the May procession in honour of Our Lady where the statue has been carried through the school grounds. It is not clear exactly when this began. There is a specific mention of it in the school magazine of 1937; "As the procession was returning we passed in front of the beautiful grotto which has been recently built under the hawthorn trees by the girls' garden."

Sylvia Jones (Mrs Jennings) remembers the procession in the 1940s, "glimpsing the reservoir through the fencing, and the girls in blue summer dresses and our veils. It was a lovely sight one doesn't forget."

Miss Eastwood recalls that on occasions "the Blessed Sacrament, exposed in monstrance, has been carried in prayerful procession around the convent area, while pupils carpeted the pathway with petals and strewn flowers, singing hymns of adoration and praise."

In addition to May, at St. Paul's October is traditionally reserved for class and lunchtime Marian devotions and reflections.

Other landmarks in the liturgical year will also be well remembered; on February 2nd a procession, each girl holding a candle, makes its way from the Old Hall to the New, for a Mass and Candlemas blessing. June sees the veneration of the Sacred Heart of Jesus, and on the Feast Day all classes reverence the Blessed Sacrament exposed on the Convent Chapel Altar. In November the dead are remembered in memorial Masses for All Souls and All Saints, with money collected for Mass offerings which have been sent, over the years to Cistercian monks at Caldey Island, African priests, Aid to the Church in need and the Oratory, the school's home parish.

School retreats and Days of Reflection are still arranged for each year group, as they have been since the beginning. Teresa Monteiro (née Bosworth) comments that these were memorable, "especially one given by a very amusing and spiritual Franciscan called Father Pascal. There was something very special about the Chapel: the smell of wax polish, candles and sometimes incense, the statues and the Stations of the Cross, and the beautiful wooden ceiling, which was painted over many years later. We had to cross the quadrangle – and ALWAYS walked in a dignified and respectful way once through that door."

Now Days of Reflection are more active, or even inter-active. The Year Seven Day, organised by Mrs Maureen May, gives pupils a chance to work in groups at St. Chad's Cathedral, learning about the hub of the diocese, participating in brass-rubbing, calligraphy and team games and helping to prepare for the daily Mass. The Year Eleven Day features outside speakers from organisations such as Life and Aquarius, while in Year Thirteen students prepare for life beyond school through reflection on how a relationship with God may be brought into the 'real' world.

There has always been a school Chaplain, but, as Sister Hilary explains, in the mid-1990s an entirely new concept of chaplaincy has been developed, as Sister Thérèse appointed the first non-priest Chaplain.

"Sr. Aileen Murphy RLR worked here as the Chaplain for six years and developed the role as it now exists. The lay Chaplain helps to prepare masses and other services, especially assemblies, and Penitential Services. She supports retreats and reflection days, either on site or in residential situations such as Savio House or Soli House (sleepless nights are part of the role!) Most importantly, she offers a listening ear to any who need extra support, need to chat about a problem, or find a shoulder to cry on. She also offers support to staff, organises the St. Vincent de Paul Society and the Young Leaders. The latter are Year Ten pupils who have successfully applied to the Leadership Project run by the Catholic Partnership. Of the Chaplains since Sister Aileen, two have been old girls of the school, Emily Rooke and the present incumbent, Stephanie Sheppard."

Steph, as she is fondly known, recalls how difficult she found this change of position at first. "I remember plucking up the courage to walk through the door into the staff room, but far worse was being expected to call the teachers

Top: The Chapel, (and panama hats) 1951.
Centre: Pilgrimage to Rome, early 1960s.
Bottom: Year 7 Retreat – the Chapel, 2006.

by their first names. Mrs May had taught me for five years and I found it hard to use her name. Then there was Miss Eastwood who had never taught me, but I was petrified of her. I needn't have worried because I was made very welcome and now I feel as if I am just one of the team."

Another recent development is the whole class reflection at the beginning of each week, known as Sacred Space. Encouraged by their form tutors, each class participates in prayer, with a notice on the door so that no-one is disturbed. During this time girls lead assemblies in turn, lighting a candle and using readings and sometimes a Power Point presentation to illustrate the theme.

Spiritual experience has never been confined within the school walls. Since the early days there have been pilgrimages, notably to Walsingham, Lourdes and Rome, as well as retreats and visits to centres like Soli House in Stratford and Alton Castle in Staffordshire. A visit by a party to Rome is recorded in the magazine of 1933 by Dorothy Ardagh-James, who particularly notes the coincidence of the school's Silver Jubilee and the Holy Year. They were able to attend an audience with the Holy Father, who blessed the party, said a few words in English and gave each one his ring to kiss. In 1937 and 1957 further visits to Rome were led by Sister Veronica, and the tradition was continued by Sr. Josephine and Sr. Agnes.

The pilgrimage to Walsingham in 1986 was a particularly memorable day because well over half the school went in a fleet of coaches. This involved a lengthy cross-country journey to Norfolk. "We thought we would never get there!" says Shinead Coyle (née Rock). Once arrived, though, the atmosphere and experience were unforgettable. Many girls walked the 'Holy Mile' barefoot, as Henry VIII had done over four centuries previously.

A party of staff and girls travelled to the Holy Land in May, 1989, visiting Lake Galilee, Capernaum, Mount Tabor, Nazareth, Cana, Masada and Jerusalem. Their first journey along the Via Dolorosa was, in the words of Miss Maureen Shaw, "exhausting and frustrating rather than uplifting", because of the commercialism and constant pestering from street-traders. However they went back the following day, led by Sister Agnes and some Belgian Sisters of the Work, who had visited Vernon Road some years before. "That day," says Miss Shaw, "the Way seemed so quiet a minor miracle seemed to be at work." She describes an early Mass next day at the Church of the Holy Sepulchre as a great highlight; "certainly words are inadequate to describe our thoughts and feelings."

For many years Miss Eastwood took groups of Sixth Formers to Caldey Island, where there was a chance to enjoy peace, and share in some of the monastic activities,

Left: Group from St. Paul's at Lourdes with Cardinal Hume, 1985.
Right: VIth form group at Lourdes, 2004.

including getting up at three o'clock for the first service of the day! On at least one occasion, Sister Agnes joined the party, and they had a particularly inclement voyage in a small boat to the island. This confirmed Sister in her long-held view that jeans were not as practical a garment as girls usually claimed, due to the length of time they took to dry following their salt water marinade!

There have been many visits to Lourdes over the years. In 2000 Miss Whelan re-introduced Year Seven to the story of Saint Bernadette and there was great eagerness on the part of the girls to join a Lourdes pilgrimage especially for their year. One recalled, "On the day you were supposed to give your money in, my cousin and I were first in the queue. Our trip to the baths was something we were, if truth be known, dreading! When we arrived we were all seated on benches and told to whisper only, while various teachers had conversations, in French, with a little man who insisted we would not be there for long. Three hours later, we had all been in the baths, and at this stage, we realised it had been worth waiting for."

The journey was by coach, and the group also visited Nevers and saw Saint Bernadette's body. Another memory was, "The journey was not particularly comfortable and at one point Father Bill and Mrs May were the only ones not suffering from travel sickness!"

The annual Diocesan Pilgrimage to Lourdes takes place during the school's half term break at the end of May. Miss Whelan, the present Head, is the Chief Handmaid of the pilgrimage. In that role she is supported by other members of staff to bring a group of girls from years 11, 12 and 13 to act as handmaids by helping serve sick pilgrims for the week. Gemma Kehoe, who left school in 2007 says, "I first went to Lourdes as a handmaid in Year 11 and found it a very rewarding experience. I went back in Year 12 and 13, and hope to continue going even though I have left school. The atmosphere in Lourdes is very special, and the friendships and relationships I formed with the sick pilgrims will stay with me forever. It wasn't all work! I had a lot of fun with the other girls and even with the teachers whom I saw in a completely different light. I would recommend the experience to anyone."

The girls have to raise over £500 each for the fare and to achieve this they pack bags in local supermarkets and hold raffles and cake sales. When in Lourdes their duties include making beds, serving meals, accompanying the sick to services and travelling with them. These students certainly do put their faith into action during that week. In 2006, Archbishop Vincent Nichols wrote to Miss Whelan, "Thank you and all associated with St. Paul's for enabling the group of girls to be part of the Diocesan pilgrimage to Lourdes."

The celebration of the school's centenary will be marked by a number of Masses and opportunities to go on pilgrimage to Walsingham, Lourdes, and for staff, a special trip to Rome.

After a hundred years the Religious Education Department, supported by the Chaplaincy team, continues to go from strength to strength, now under the leadership of Miss Eastwood's long-time disciple, Miss Margaret Czepiel, herself a former pupil. An Inspection was carried out by the Archdiocese of Birmingham in April, 2007. At the time the four Young Leaders who had been chosen to go on the Catholic Partnership Leadership course had just returned. Before the school was notified of the inspection, Mia Archer, Aine Murphy, Abbey Randall and Sarah Tuohey had planned a project for Year Seven involving team building games and a Mass in the Chapel. Having complete faith in the four girls, it was decided they should go ahead, and the team of inspectors were most impressed by their leadership qualities, organisational skills and commitment to the spiritual life of the school. The Inspection report summed up its findings: "The R.E. Department is at the forefront and makes an outstanding contribution to its (the school's) overall life… the quality of teaching and learning are outstanding."

In the words of Claire Eastwood:

"Prayer, worship and liturgical celebrations are at the heart of the Catholic faith and tradition, and in St. Paul's, are the experiences through which the community may pray with their life, and make of their life and prayer a praise offering to God. In the education of the whole person, St. Paul's has proudly promoted and faithfully fostered a living liturgy, so that the faith community may hear the Lord call their name."

The testimony of many former pupils echoes Miss Eastwood's description of a living liturgy in a community where faith is not confined within a chapel or an R.E. classroom. It is well summed up by Mary Levesley (née Cusack), a pupil from 1953–1959.

"I learned things on the syllabus so I knew I was learning. I didn't realise that I was learning lots of other things by osmosis, things I would not be aware of until years later. This learning came from those sometimes incidental acts of care, kindness, that were offered to me and others by a range of people involved in educating us.

"They were leading me out towards another way of living my life… they gave me practical demonstrations of the meaning of charity. They had a care for me because I was a child who needed care – even if I didn't know it – even when I made it difficult for them.

"I recently attended yet another training day for my work as a counsellor. At one point we were asked to imagine ourselves back in our childhoods; it was suggested that if this was disturbing we should take ourselves to a place of safety, somewhere where we had good memories. I spent some of the exercise in my own private asylum; back in that place of safety that for me was St. Paul's High School for Girls in the 1950s."

Chapter 10

THE COMPREHENSIVE SCHOOL (1974–1990)

In September, 1974, Sr. Marie Agnes took on the Headship of the School and the task of overseeing its transition from selective grammar to comprehensive. She was particularly suited to this enterprise, being an energetic and forceful lady who was always ready to embrace change and challenge, while strictly upholding the school's traditional values and ethos.

Form Vs, 1979.

Under 13 Hockey Team, 1983.

The first big occasion for the school that term was the visit of Mother Teresa of Calcutta on September 12th, 1974. As the renovation of the main Hall was under way, the whole school crowded into the Old Hall, with the Sixth Form craning through the Upper Corridor windows to get a view of the small white-clad figure whose presence carried such power. The atmosphere was well-described in the newsletter of the co-workers of Mother Teresa:

"We made our way to St. Paul's Convent, Birmingham, for lunch, followed by a visit to the attached Grammar School where Mother made a tremendous impact. One moment the hundreds of girls were chattering like magpies, the next moment when they realised Mother was there, you could have heard the proverbial pin drop. Then came the applause, the smiles, the rapt attention while Mother addressed them, then more applause. Flowers were presented, in fact Mother's path seemed to be strewn with flowers that day."

Margaret Czepiel, then in third year (Year 9), remembers describing the occasion to herself more succinctly: "Wow! I've met a saint!"

Jackie Parkes (née Smyth) was a new girl that year. At the date of writing in 2007, she has five daughters in school, one who went on from St. Paul's to study medicine, and two still to come!

Sports Day, c. 1986.

"I started St. Paul's in September, 1974. I thought I had entered Heaven, or the Enid Blyton school of my dreams. Growing up in Sparkbrook and educated in inner-city Birmingham at St. Anne's School in Digbeth, there was quite a culture shock. You see, we had felt outdoor hats and brown indoor shoes. All this still in 1974!"

Change, as ever, was afoot, though, and preparations went ahead throughout 1974–75 for the school to embrace its new comprehensive status. Various different curricula and teaching methods were studied, and advisers and practitioners came to deliver training to prepare for the new wider intake of pupils. A memorable day was in June, 1975, when the girls had a holiday, and the whole staff decamped to St. Paul's College at Newbold Revell for a training day, studying mixed ability teaching methods. The first person to greet them, with great affection, was Sister Josephine, who, far from being retired, was lecturing at the College.

Building work to repair and replace the fire-damaged hall and classrooms went on until early in 1979. The Sixth Form never really regained their common room, but there was a spacious new room for Music, and the Art and Craft Department gained accommodation on the top floor. The well in the centre of the building, between the original structure and the 1960s Science labs was reduced in size but

Lacrosse — prefab and convent in rear.

enhanced by the construction of a pond, by Mr John Mellor, Head of Geography, who also maintained a weather station in this area. Generations of ducks came to the pond, flying in from the reservoir, and in springtime little processions of ducklings were a great attraction for the girls. Unfortunately they were also extremely attractive to marauding hordes of magpies. Pupils from that era will perhaps remember that Mr Mellor, in addition to his many talents, was a man of sporting interests, and from time to time there was decimation of the magpie predators.

Sister Agnes proved even more adept than her predecessors at finding possibilities previously unthought of for conversion of parts of the building. There was further use of the rooms in the convent where the preparatory section had been, mostly to house the Business Studies and Information Technology departments, which grew rapidly in the late 1970s and 1980s, and are now such an important part of the school.

During this period there continued to be great continuity of staffing, but inevitably there were changes. Miss Mary Smith retired as Deputy Head and was succeeded by Mrs Dympna Morby (née Taylor), another former pupil. As St. Paul's grew to a four and then a five form entry school, the task of managing it grew ever more complex and demanding. In recognition of this, a second Deputy, also a former pupil, Miss Mary Holland, was appointed in 1980.

In the summer of that year two very long-serving members of staff, Miss Betty Steward (Classics) and Mrs K. (Edie) Samuel (Maths) retired. Mrs Samuel was one of the real characters on the staff. She was remembered by Clare Short (M.P. for Ladywood) in an article in the *Times Educational Supplement* in 1996.

"She and I used to compete to get shorter proofs for the geometry theorems and I really rather liked her... she would put a theorem on the board and I would say, 'I can do it shorter'. And she would groan and write mine up, and then figure out a way to make hers shorter. We had a sort of friendly, slightly competitive relationship."

No sooner had the school weathered the change from Grammar to Comprehensive than discussions began in the City and in the Catholic school sector about possible reorganisation and co-operation at Sixth Form level. Much time was spent in meetings and discussions, notably with Blessed Humphrey Middlemore and Cardinal Newman schools, but essentially St. Paul's continued as it was. (Sadly the two aforementioned schools have since been demolished and are now the site of housing developments).

The era of House plays had ended with the decline of the House system in all schools including St. Paul's, but this was a particularly flourishing time for school productions, especially the memorable Gilbert and Sullivan light operas produced by Miss Wilson, which are described in detail in a separate chapter.

Other plays were produced at Christmas and ends of term by Mrs Morby (*The Servant of Two Masters* was memorable), Mrs Simpson (*The Stars are Dancing*), and towards the end of the 1980s by Mr Kevin Kelly (who not only directed *Smike*, but made a fearsome Wackford Squeers). Although the stage in the New Hall is a large one, the professional standards achieved were all the more creditable considering the limitations of space backstage, with no greenroom, and large choruses and casts having to be dressed and made up in an adjacent classroom, and then marshalled on and off stage. Spare a thought, too, for those heroic volunteers who kept the offstage actors quiet and occupied in the gym, often shivering with nerves, and cold!

A different, but no less enjoyable production of the mid-80s was the staff pantomime, *Persil White and the Seven Dwarves*, drawing ostensibly on the tale of Snow White, but incorporating strands from other traditional pantos like *Aladdin*, *Cinderella* and *Goldilocks and the Three Bears*. So successfully did this play to a cheering audience of the whole school that it was fixed in the collective staff memory, and was revived with some topical additions in 1992, and then extensively updated in 2004. Few who saw the first version will forget Mr Mellor's stentorian turn as The Mirror, the collective gambolling of the P.E. Department as the three bears, various normally

Top left: Irish Dancers, 1967. Top right: The Stars Are Dancing, Christmas 1986.
Bottom left: Vietnamese Hat Dance, Christmas 1986.
Bottom right: Liturgical Dance group, 1985.

petite ladies in tunics stuffed with cushions to impersonate the seven dwarves, and the late entrance of the Art Department (Alan and Nina Grove) as the Pantomime Horse. In a nod to a recent addition to the Royal Family, the Prince was not Charming but Harry, spiritedly undertaken by Mrs Val Reynolds of Business Studies.

Mrs Shinead Coyle, now Head of History, then Shinead Rock, remembers how at the end of the pantomime "masked kidnappers appeared at each door of the New Hall, and Sister Agnes was stolen away, only to be returned when a ransom demand had been paid. I remember everybody turning out their pockets and doing their bit to make sure that Sister was safely returned to us."

Dance was a particular feature of many productions and also of liturgy in the school at this time, especially under the directorship of Miss Frankie Capaldi. There also continued to be a strong tradition of Irish dancing, with many girls bringing the expertise gained in local dance schools into St. Paul's. As the school grew in diversity to represent the increasingly multicultural community on its doorstep, other cultural strands emerged, especially in the beautiful Vietnamese dances with fans, candles and hats which graced several concerts and entertainments.

The first two Vietnamese pupils joined St. Paul's in October, 1982 and they soon grew into a sizable community. Throughout its life the school has gained a lot from various ethnic groups, notably at first the Irish, Polish, Ukrainians and Italians. The Vietnamese arrived in Birmingham in the late 1970s, part of the migration known as the Boat People. There has continued to be a significant number of girls with Afro-Caribbean roots, and also from the various Asian communities including many Muslim girls who have joined St. Paul's Sixth Form from Selly Park and Bordesley Green Girls' Schools, among others.

In May, 1985 this diverse heritage was celebrated in a Multicultural Mass, a very large event in the school's history. Miss Dawn Casserly, the present Deputy Head and then a pupil remembers it vividly.

"The rehearsals were like a modern day version of the Tower of Babel, with everyone practising their parts of the Mass in their own languages – French, German, Russian, Polish, Vietnamese, Italian, Irish, Urdu, Spanish, etc. How God was ever going to make sense of any of this was beyond me! Yet there was a profound message that, although everyone had a different culture, language, music and dance, we all belonged to the One Father, the God of All Nations and All Peoples.

"The Mass, while it highlighted our diversity, also confirmed our common identity, faith heritage and tradition that we all shared in school; and we knew that although we might never be able to speak our friend's language, or dance with the grace and elegance of the Vietnamese, we would always be united, and take huge pride in being 'St. Paul's girls'."

Public Speaking and debating flourished from the early 1970s, with teams finding success in competitions organised by the Knights of St. Columba, the Catenians and the Business and Professional Women's Guild among others. In 1976, Tina McKevitt and Clare Murphy won the Douglas Maine Nicholls Trophy in a debating competition organised by the Birmingham and Midland Institute, a feat repeated in 1988 by Patricia McTigue and Deirdre Collins. From 1979 the school has held its own annual public-speaking competition, organised by the English Department, with class rounds leading to a grand final at the end of the summer term. The tradition has expanded with the advent of an annual debating competition between the schools of the Catholic Partnership.

Miss Jordan presented with Bene Merenti medal, 1986.

In July 1986, Miss Philippa Jordan retired as Head of History after 32 years service to the school. Like her mother and sisters she is a former pupil. In November of that year friends, colleagues and relatives gathered for Mass in the Convent chapel, at which Philippa was presented with the Bene Merenti medal in recognition of her outstanding service. Teresa Monteiro (née Bosworth), at school in the 50s, remembers Miss Jordan as "a firm favourite. She was quiet, interesting and amusing. There was always a large history group in the Sixth Form because she was so popular." She also recalls Miss Jordan's sensitivity: "she could often be seen quietly listening to some girl in difficulties, with her head slightly on one side, occasionally making a wise and appropriate comment."

The following year saw the retirement of other long-serving teachers, Miss Maureen Shaw (English and History), Miss Angela Clarkson (French) and Sister Catherine Murphy, Head of Home Economics and familiar to girls of an earlier era as "Sister Baptist". As Head of Domestic Science, later Home Economics, and Head of Sixth Form, Sister Catherine was a central figure in all school activities, and her experience and wisdom were widely drawn on by successive Heads and senior staff. When hospitality was required for guests, inspectors or evening functions, it was

Left: Sr. Catherine cuts her retirement cake. Top right: Miss Angela Clarkson.
Bottom right: Miss Maureen Shaw. All at their retirement party, 1987.

Sister Catherine and her team who provided everything from melt-in-the-mouth canapés to three course dinners. Among Sister's many talents was the production of gorgeous cakes and trifles for staff buffets and farewell teas; the trifles were so strongly laced with sherry as to raise conviviality at these functions to a very high level!

One of the great strengths of St. Paul's has been its ability to maintain high traditional standards while embracing innovations in educational thinking and practice. This was never more true than in the mid-1980s when the school was particularly closely involved in two city-wide initiatives; CREST (Creativity in Science and Technology) and TRIST (Teacher-Related In-Service Training). (We also became very practised in the use of acronyms, then as now!) These involved St. Paul's in exciting developments in team teaching and student-centred learning, among them Alan and Nina Grove's papermaking enterprise, and the making of musical instruments.

With so much collaborative work going on, schools were encouraged under the Technical and Vocational Education Initiative (TVEI) to group together to pool strengths and training opportunities. From this was born the Birmingham Catholic Partnership, which continues, long after other partnerships faded, to be a vibrant organisation providing valuable training opportunities for staff in all subjects, and the chance for pupils from the different schools to participate in all kinds of activities. Its inaugural meeting was on the September 18th, 1987 and at that time it consisted of St. Paul's, St. Philip's College, St. Thomas Aquinas, St. John Wall, Bishop Challoner, Archbishop Ilsley, Cardinal Newman, Cardinal Wiseman and Holy Trinity Schools. Later other schools were co-opted. The first co-ordinator was Mr Jim Foley, who later became Head of St. Thomas Aquinas. Later in the 1990s with the Partnership going from strength to strength and recognised nationally as a model for school collaboration, Miss Cathy Feeney, an old girl of St. Paul's and then a Senior Teacher, was appointed to the co-ordinatorship, a post she holds today.

St. Paul's work in the Partnership was co-ordinated in the early days by Mrs Helen Goodwin, who was extremely energetic and adept at disseminating new ideas and practice, and leading staff to make the most of current educational initiatives.

Cathy Hynes with Duke of Edinburgh group including Prince Edward, 1986.

After moving on to Headship in the South, Helen has returned to the Midlands, and it seems most fitting that she is now Head at Cardinal Wiseman School in Coventry, which has close connections with St. Paul's. Sister Francis Clare Aylward was Head there previously. As Superior of the Convent at Vernon Road and a Governor for many years, she is a great friend to the school.

Extra-curricular activities and trips flourished. Most were greatly enjoyed but one sad event which happened on a Duke of Edinburgh Bronze Expedition to the centre at Sharpness in February 1983 was the very sudden death of Jayne Vassallo, a Year 10 pupil. This was a great shock and Jayne was deeply mourned by her classmates and the whole school.

Left to right: Maureen Mannion, Mary Chilton and Joanna Hawan. 1st Duke of Edinburgh Gold Award winners, 1976.

With Sister Agnes's support and encouragement, the Duke of Edinburgh's Award Scheme continued to be an important activity in school, involving many girls and various staff members, especially Sister Helena, Sister Hilary and Miss Sheila Armstrong, often to be seen on a Friday afternoon amassing tents and equipment for weekend expeditions. Cathy Hynes remembers a day in January, 1986, when she was chosen to take part in an expedition to the Shropshire hills involving a televised interview with Prince Edward. There were some amusing moments in this adventure, including the appearance of the Prince's bodyguards in lounge suits and lace-up shoes. After a couple of hours struggling up the hill in very poor weather they resembled snowmen. "Eventually we began the descent to warmer territory, stumbling, slipping and sliding downwards. Chatting with the Prince about the Award and the day's activities, I tried to act as though a royal conversation was commonplace.

"My favourite part of each Award was always the expeditions and packing a rucksack was always a problem, though carrying it was less of a struggle. However on a blustery, cold day in Shropshire, when Prince Edward, in true chivalrous style, offered to carry my rucksack for me, I accepted with glee and handed over the cumbersome load. What a great day!"

There were ski-trips to Italy, Modern Languages Department trips to France and several journeys with the Classical Studies Department to Greece, led by Miss Mary Holland and Sister Hilary. Miss Holland recalls other activities of their department in the 1980s and 90s.

"Latin was included on the timetable from the school's early days, but once it was no longer required for university entrance, its status was reduced. Consequently in the early 1980s it was phased out. By this time Classical Studies or Classical Literature in Translation was becoming a popular option as it was accessible to a wider range of abilities. The stories from ancient Greece or Rome lent themselves to a variety of interpretations to be explored enthusiastically by members of Lower School, whether it be composing poems or plays, creating works of art such as Medusa masks, acting out dramas or making models of theatres or temples.

"A highlight of the year in the 80s and 90s was the Classical Studies Day, organised by Sister Hilary and Miss Holland. All of the Lower School participated in one way or another. Each class staged a dramatic performance of one of the stories they had studied: perhaps Orpheus in search of his beloved Eurydice, Perseus in quest of the Medusa's head, Persephone being swept away to the Underworld by Hades, or Pyramus dying tragically in the arms of Thisbe, to name just a few. The enthusiasm

Classical Studies Day – Theseus and the Minotaur.

Masks – for Classical Studies Day.

was catching as the dramas unfolded. Part of the fun was dressing up for the occasion. Sister Hilary always had a box of props and costumes, providing cloaks and tunics, crowns, goblets, swords and even a donkey from Majorca! The girls always seemed to find just the right additions for their costumes. The third years were more ambitious and gave some serious and convincing performances of *King Oedipus* or amused everyone with their antics in excerpts from an Aristophanes comedy such as *The Frogs* or *The Wasps*. Hours of rehearsals were put in beforehand; the plays always turned out fine on the day and Miss Holland would video the performances, which were eagerly watched afterwards."

In October, 1988, the school celebrated its eightieth anniversary. Sister Maria Rosa, Superior-General of the Sisters of St. Paul of Charity, speaking at the commemorative Mass, quoted the words of Jacob Riis the sociologist.

"When nothing seems to help, I go and look at a stone-cutter hammering away at a rock, perhaps a hundred times, without so much as a crack showing. Yet at the hundred and first blow it will split in two, and I know it was not that blow that did it, but all that had gone before."

"So, today," she continued, "we celebrate the ALL that has gone before and the ALL that is to come."

Left: Fire Quiz winners, 1988. Right: Sixth Form, 1987.

One very large thing to come was the school's connection with Romania, which began shortly before Sr. Agnes's retirement, when Mrs Anne Harris and Miss Geraldine Brown (now Mrs McCauley) of the English Department joined a group from the Catholic Partnership taking clothes and supplies to an orphanage in Siret, in Romania. The country was newly accessible after the fall of the dictator, Ceausescu, in December, 1989, and already it was apparent that thousands of orphans and unwanted children were living in very deprived and even sordid circumstances.

When Anne and Geraldine returned, just before the end of the summer term in 1990, they told the school about all they had seen and experienced in a special assembly. Their revelations shocked and moved girls and staff, many shedding tears at the plight of the children. The scenes of deprivation at Siret were broadcast in the "Challenge Anneka" television programme later that year, when Geraldine Brown and a colleague from St. Thomas Aquinas School, Monica McDaid, enlisted the help of the BBC in beginning a programme of renovation and rehabilitation of the orphanage and its children.

Although by that time Sr. Agnes had retired from the Headship of St. Paul's she went on to strengthen and deepen the school's links with Romania, going at first to the Colentina Hospital in Bucharest with her friend Sister Cyril, and there nursing AIDS babies. The Archbishop of Bucharest discovered them and asked them to set up a summer school at Campalung in the Carpathian foothills, for older high school students to learn English. From November, 1991, Sister became involved with setting up houses in Bucharest for street children from orphanages and broken homes. Many of these were runaways who had been living rough, sleeping in parks, sewers and ventilation shafts. As time went on an outpost of the Congregation was established with a novitiate.

Left: Staff, 1987. Right: Three Heads, Sr. Agnes, Sr. Thérèse, Sr. Josephine, early 1990s.

It was typical of Sister Agnes that "retirement" was in fact the beginning of a new and strenuous challenge. Her work in Romania inspired pupils and staff at St. Paul's to many fund-raising efforts, and in some cases to spend time working over there in holidays.

Like all its other Heads, Sr. Agnes left an indelible impression on the school and indeed on all who met her. One was never in doubt of what she was thinking – she would breeze into the staff room either to share good news with enthusiasm, or to tell us where St. Paul's had sunk to that morning as a result of the misdemeanour of some pupil. She was not a lady you argued with, so it was well that she was wise and far-seeing in her vision for the school. She wanted everything to do with school to be perfect, sitting for hours at rehearsals of concerts and operas, and sometimes taking charge to fire up a sluggish performance or make an adjustment to a costume. She was supportive of all extra-curricular activities, attending matches, debates and competitions to cheer on the pupils.

With all this, Sister Agnes was an extremely kind and warm-hearted person, always ready to sympathise with and accommodate staff or pupils with problems, especially where there was family illness or misfortune. Her connection with the school remained strong throughout her years in Romania, and she was thrilled with the enthusiastic efforts made to raise money for her work there. The huge gathering at her funeral in July 2006 attested to the universal affection and respect in which she was held, and although naturally a sad farewell, the occasion was also a chance for friends to celebrate their memories of an exciting time at St. Paul's, as well as a remarkable life of service.

Chapter 11

MUSIC AND DRAMA (1961–2008)

From the early days of the Choir to the joint St. Paul's–St. Philip's productions of the post-war years, the school had already established a strong tradition of music and drama. This has flourished and grown over the second half of the school's history.

Miss Kathleen Hermolle a past pupil was Head of Music from 1961, succeeding Miss Mayes, and has kindly supplied her recollections below.

★ ★ ★ ★ ★

SWEET SOUNDS OF THE SIXTIES

It was something of a shock to arrive for my first day of teaching at St. Paul's to discover that the only equipment was a wind-up gramophone and some old '78' records. The only instruments were the Weimar grand piano in the Hall, an old upright in the gym, and in one of the classrooms. I was told I had to ask the School Secretary, Sister Gertrude, for anything I wanted. So I bravely set off to ask for a record-player. In no uncertain terms I was told that the French Department already had one, as did the P.E. Department. We couldn't have another! St. Paul's became the only school where I tendered my resignation during my first term.

Sister Ethelbert, pouring oil on troubled waters, sent for a tray of tea and biscuits and persuaded me that, in time, when funds became available, I should get some equipment, and of course, in time I did.

A rather amusing experience occurred in my first term. Having decided to put on a Christmas choir concert, I got copies of Britten's *Ceremony of Carols* for the purpose. About half-way through rehearsals, half the choir left, saying they had never sung anything like this before. The rest of us continued and eventually put on a moderately successful performance. We ultimately achieved quite a reputation for singing Benjamin Britten's works. On the occasion of a visit to the school by the great actress, Dame Sybil Thorndike, she asked if the choir could sing anything for her. A hasty message to St. Philip's produced John Steward, the Maths teacher, to play the organ accompaniment. The whole school assembled in our new hall, equipped with a small, two manual, Walker pipe organ (the result of funds raised by several garden fêtes, much hard work and merriment) and Britten's *Missa Brevis* was performed. At the finish I was given a great 'bear hug' by Dame Sybil, who was clearly delighted with the spontaneity of the beautiful singing.

The new buildings of the sixties included a Music Room. This led to a phone call from the City Music Adviser to the effect that I could have a new piano. 'Lovely,' I said, 'but more benefit to me than the pupils. Now if that money was spent, instead, on orchestral instruments, free tuition from the City peripatetic instrumentalists would be available to the girls'.

Mr Adams said he would have to think about this. Some days later he rang to agree. Our new instruments led to the formation of our embryonic orchestra and various new musical experiences.

By the end of the decade, successful O and A-level courses were well-established. Nevertheless, singing remained of the utmost importance. Mozart's *Ave Verum* became something of a school anthem, sometimes replacing a hymn when the whole school would harmonise it at assembly. A Music Club was formed, at which visiting choirs, orchestras and soloists took part. These were evening events so that parents, as well as pupils, could come, free of charge. Generally we had a splendid and appreciative audience. It also provided a further platform for our Senior, Junior and Madrigal choirs, as did many of our less formal school concerts.

Because of their performances, the choir became known and we received invitations to do recitals in St. Edward's; St. Catherine's in the Horsefair; at City Church, Oxford; for the Ockenden Venture; a broadcast recital for BBC Midlands and to take part in music on TV on Christmas morning, among others. At the end of a concert I was invariably asked, 'When is our next concert, Miss Hermolle?' For one thing, my mother always baked a huge batch of her famous cakes for the choir to eat during the interval between rehearsal and performance!

On April 1st, 1969, the Senior Choir made a record which still gives me great enjoyment and happy memories.

★ ★ ★ ★ ★

Miss Kathleen Hermolle was succeeded initially by Mr Christopher Morley, familiar to many Midlanders as Music Critic of the *Birmingham Post*, and then in 1974 by Miss Margaret Wilson. In 1979 Miss Wilson took on the tremendous task of producing *Iolanthe*, first in a series of memorable Gilbert and Sullivan productions. Her own old school, Heanor Grammar in Derbyshire, had a great tradition of producing a G&S opera each year, and she relished the idea of giving her pupils a similar experience.

Miss Wilson remembers great support and teamwork from the staff, but she herself did all the stage direction and dialogue rehearsals as well as the music, not to mention the flowers. The task was even more mammoth as there was so much interest in the project, and talent in the school, that it was decided to have a double cast of principals. Miss Wilson remembers persuading a friend to make the stage set which was beautifully painted by Miss Blackband, while Sister Catherine and her team made enchanting costumes for the Peers and Fairies.

The next production, in 1980, was *The Pirates of Penzance*. Ruth Stokes (née Branson) was a pirate. "I remember the lovely black teeth paint we wore. I always played a male role in the productions, probably because of my alto voice. It's odd now, whenever I listen to Gilbert and Sullivan, I always sing along with the male harmony parts!"

Ruth also particularly recalls the impact of the real male voices of Mr David Henson (then Head of Music at St. Thomas Aquinas) and Mr John Meyrick, who took lead parts in most of the productions, and added an extra depth and dimension to the sound. David Henson, busy with his own department, was notorious for learning lines only just in the nick of time. Sometimes he missed a cue, but the resourceful orchestra ad-libbed an extra verse. Ruth's memory of Mr Meyrick is of "a lovely gentleman who always seemed to be smiling."

Yeomen of the Guard, in 1981, was the first G&S production to have an orchestral accompaniment. "This added a little bit more stress!" says Margaret Wilson. "The girls did us proud, and the unaccompanied quartet *Sing a Merry Madrigal* sticks in my mind."

The last in the series was *The Mikado*, with Michelle de Souza outstanding in the main 'patter' part. In addition to these mammoth productions there was usually a big Christmas concert which, for Margaret Wilson are also treasured memories.

"Choirs, vocal and instrumental soloists, Wind Bands, Flute Choirs, Clarinet and Brass ensembles as well as a huge orchestra… No player was ever turned away and we managed to arrange special parts when needed – harp, tuba, even a part for beginner violin players using open string and one finger for the Hallelujah Chorus one year!

"Though final rehearsals were highly pressured, we achieved such a shared sense of purpose, enthusiasm, respect and group responsibility that the smooth running of the day was ensured. The visit of the head on these occasions to give us the final seal of approval confirmed the mutual respect felt by everyone. Wonderful refreshments made by the H.E. department for the guests in the interval were a highlight also. Sisters, Governors, former staff and friends were invited and gave an added importance to every performance. In the very early days there might be at least three former Music teachers present, and this was always very special. These days summed up the ethos of St. Paul's for me."

Margaret remembers the early 90s as a particularly fertile time for choral singing at St. Paul's. Many girls became involved also in the City of Birmingham Youth Choruses. Special highlights included the 1995 summer Concert in the Old Hall, with St. Paul's Choir, Melisma (the chamber choir of which Margaret herself was a founding member) and Dympna Morby, always a charismatic speaker, reminiscing about her memories of St. Paul's. In 1998 the Chorale gave a very inspiring recital in the chapel, and sang for the Head Teachers' Conference in Birmingham. Two talented singers from this period were Julia Campbell (who took the title part in *Ebeneezer*) and her friend Katrina Dodd.

One result of Margaret Wilson's connection with the CBSO Chorus was that the orchestra rehearsed in school at the time when Sir Simon Rattle was their conductor. He signed a sheet of paper to wish everyone in the Music Department Good Luck! It was framed and still holds pride of place. Ruth Stokes remembers, "One piece of music they played was a spring scene, and just as the orchestra paused, the birds outside broke into a loud burst of singing – it was magical!"

While the Choir and musicians were flourishing, Drama was expanding in the 90s as a curriculum subject, and also in stage productions under the capable direction of Miss Beverley Chapple (later Mrs Dunne), ably assisted by Miss Diana Thomas, who eventually succeeded her.

Beverley remembers that during her time at St. Paul's, she was delighted to set up the Drama studio, having been teaching in a room that had previously been full of typewriters. "The department was able to splash out on a lighting desk, blackout curtains and stage lights, a far cry from the 'typing pool' where they used to look out at the baby ducklings.

"Speaking of lighting, I remember the time I thought a death had happened on stage! When I first arrived at St. Paul's there was a very old-fashioned stage lighting system that didn't work properly, and I recall asking Mr Hynes (a good neighbour of the school who was an electrician) to have a little look at it. I remember standing on the stage near the orange velvet curtains and Mr Hynes disappeared from view. Then I heard this dreadful sizzling sound, an 'Aargh!' and a loud thud. Mr Hynes had electrocuted himself! I was so scared he'd done himself some serious damage. It went quiet and nothing moved for a few seconds. Then I plucked up courage to peep around the curtain, expecting the worst. It was okay – Mr Hynes wasn't dead! He had, however, burnt his hand quite badly. It was a lucky escape. I remember scurrying off to the staff room afterwards and I was so pale and shaky that Miss Eastwood had to make me a cup of sugary, sweet tea!"

Mr Hynes will be remembered by many, especially on the staff, as indeed a very good friend and neighbour from across Vernon Road, not to mention as the parent of Celine, Bernadette, Cathy and Thérèse, all former pupils.

The new lighting was obviously a great improvement. *The Greatest Show on Earth*, with a circus theme was a very successful production. Miss Chapple and Miss Geraldine Brown then worked together to produce *A Midsummer Night's Dream*, a magical summer experience, in July, 1993.

Ebeneezer, in 1995, a musical version of *A Christmas Carol*, was a joint production for the Music and Drama departments, with Julia Campbell in the title role. It won the Knights of St. Columba trophy for the best school production of the year in Birmingham. This was followed in 1996 by *Charlie and the Chocolate Factory*, with a huge and enthusiastic chorus of Oompa-Loompas.

Beverley Dunne particularly remembers the "fantastic set designs for these big productions created by Peter Wells, a very gifted generous man who gave up so much time to build them. The shows definitely would not have been the same without his creative insight and genius for turning plywood into a work of art."

One of Beverley's main aims was to get girls producing theatre for live audiences in the community. As part of GCSE work puppet shows were taken to the Oratory, *The Wizard of Oz* to Longwill School for the Deaf, and a version of *Cinderella* to Calthorpe Special School. Christmas was 'done' in as many ways as possible: "using giant puppets to retell the Nativity; we also had talking Christmas trees, shepherds dressed as builders and drunken revellers, not forgetting talking toys, spoilt children and frustrated parents."

In the post-Millennium years a new musical drama production team, Mrs Suzanne Markovics and Miss Diana Thomas took over the stage with some very energetic and effervescent productions. Suzanne Markovics remembers *Bugsy Malone* as being very special in that it was her first musical at St. Paul's. "There was a fantastic

Left: Ebeneezer, Christmas 1995.
Right: The Dracula Spectacula – Musical Production, 2006.

cast, notably Mwenya Kawesha as Fat Sam, Rebecca Harris as Tallulah and Maya Motamedi, who sang her solos as Blousey Brown with real panache. There were some wonderful visual/dramatic effects through the direction of Miss Diana Thomas, and a committed and talented band for the accompaniment."

Mrs Markovics has encouraged the proliferation of vocal and instrumental ensembles from Gospel Choir to String ensemble; from Chamber Choir to Wind band and from Irish group to Recorders, led by an old friend to St. Paul's music, Mr Tony White. A very special project in 2007 has been the formation of a Centenary Choir, under the direction of Mr David Lawrence. It is clear to anyone attending school concerts that a greater number than ever of girls are being encouraged and enabled to participate in music-making.

In 2006 the school put on one of the liveliest productions ever – *The Dracula Spectacula*, with "a very motivated and professional cast, a joy to work with. Noteworthy performances came from across the cast, particularly Dracula (Onyojah Momoh), Wraith (Jessica Sutton) and Genghis (Debbie-Anne O'Neill) in their top hat and cane dance routine, A Super Rat like Me. The Chorus of 'Idiots' did some fabulous routines in a number of areas of the production, and Lucy Price won a Knights of St. Columba award for a showstopping performance in the role of Gretel."

Dao Nguyen played one of the main characters, and she recalls, "The show incorporated pupils from every year group. We spent many hours after school and on Sundays doing rehearsals. All the hard work and dedication paid off, as we won the Commended Award in the Knights of St. Columba competition. It was a fantastic show and we all had a great time."

In addition to the performances and concerts for special occasions, both Music and Drama are now very important and established curriculum subjects with excellent results in public examinations, and growing each year in the numbers of candidates. Both have been involved in the Creative Partnership Scheme, and St. Paul's has now been awarded a Silver Arts Mark Award for its development of Creative Arts. The traditions begun by Father Robert and Miss Mayes, among many others, have clearly endured and flourished, and evoke many happy memories wherever St. Paul's girls meet.

Chapter 12

BUILDING ON TRADITION
(1990–1999)

In September, 1990 Sister Thérèse Browne took up the Headship of St. Paul's. Like her predecessors, she combined a regard for the school's traditional standards of excellence with a desire to build on them and embrace change wherever it could benefit the students. By now the school had expanded to a six-form entry comprehensive of close on 1000 students, much the same number as today. In addition to the traditional subjects, there were flourishing departments of Drama, Craft, Design and Technology, Business Studies, Information Technology and Sociology.

A major problem, and not a new one, was that while the school was flourishing, the building was getting very cramped, even despite Sister Agnes's energy and ingenuity in making use of space. However, before her retirement, further building work was carried out at the back of the main school building to add additional science laboratories on top of the existing Chemistry and Physics laboratories. These were opened in 1991, one of the principal guests at the opening being former pupil Sally Hay, (Mrs Sally Burton). Later, a new Drama studio was added on this upper floor.

Earlier that year, in July, Mrs Dympna Morby (née Taylor) retired as Deputy Head after sixteen years. A lady of huge charm and energy, she was a charismatic teacher of English, especially fondly remembered by her A-level students. They found her enthusiasm for literature inspiring, remembering particularly her teaching of twentieth century writers as diverse as Graham Greene, Sean O'Casey and Philip Larkin. She contributed greatly to the dramatic life of the school, producing a variety of plays and entertainments. How she found time and energy for this in addition to her teaching and management duties is still a joyful mystery. Dympna Morby was the most approachable of Deputy Heads, with a wonderful talent for making others feel good about themselves and thus spurring them on to greater achievements. A favourite with staff and girls alike, she was nevertheless adept at keeping everyone on their toes. Staff lingering a little too long after break in cosy corners of the staff room were reminded of their duties with a crisp "Ladies and gentlemen, the bell has rung." However on feast days and sometimes simply when she thought staff needed a treat, hers was a generous hand with a glass of wine or sherry, just when it was most needed to perk up flagging spirits.

After her retirement, Dympna spent a lot of time fund-raising for Romania, and working there with Sister Agnes, especially in the summer school at Campalung. Their friendship continued until Sister Agnes's death, and it was fitting that Dympna Morby was at her bedside then.

The school had never recovered the Sixth Form accommodation destroyed by the fire of 1974, which had provided small group seminar rooms, a language laboratory and a spacious Common Room. The Upper Sixth after that had their common room in an L-shaped room between the New Hall and the Music Room. It was very cramped and the shape meant that tutors taking assemblies were unable to see the whole group (possibly sometimes an advantage for the wearier students in the corner who had a chance to drop off or chat amongst themselves!) The Lower Sixth Common Room was much bigger, being in a freestanding 'temporary' prefab (it was actually in use for over 30 years). It was prone to draughts and leaks and was once the scene of a dramatic incident when the roof, in the process of being retarred, caught fire, and although it was a separate building, the whole school had to troop out onto the field and stay there till the Fire Brigade arrived.

Now again in 1991, with large Sixth Form numbers and an awareness that these must be maintained, the Sisters came to the rescue and it was agreed that the rear quarter of the Convent building should become a Sixth Form Centre, accessed from that part of the building which had been used by the school since the days of the preparatory department. This provided both small group teaching rooms and two common rooms, and was opened by Bishop Pargeter at a Mass and inaugural ceremony in December, 1991.

Another 'grand opening' was in October, 1993 when Dennis Stewart (Olympic Bronze in Judo) and Laura Branchard of the Canadian Olympic hockey team opened the Health Studio and Sauna after refurbishment of the original room which had been in use since 1989.

The school was now a great deal larger. The original building was more than double its original size, there were extra classrooms in the convent together with the Sixth Form accommodation, and by 1993 there were eleven classrooms in prefabricated buildings behind the Convent. Yet there still never seemed to be enough space. When examinations were being held in the New Hall (and at times the gym), assemblies were held in the Old Hall. Even with different groups using it on a rota basis it still seemed crowded.

Mrs Djukic's wedding reception,
Old Hall.

Sarah Simmons (who later returned to St. Paul's to teach History) found it a trial. "The Old Hall was horrendous, all squashed in... how many people fainted? I was one of them, whisked off on a number of occasions after falling flat on my face. The privilege was to have a chair to sit on, if assembly was in the New Hall. The trouble was that Sixth Formers would stand in front of you and prevent air getting to you, and by the time Miss Wilson had made you "sing properly", you were near to fainting on the chair as well!"

"Singing properly" seems to have been a perennial issue for St. Paul's as well as other schools. Bernadette Shortt remembers Miss Casserly and Miss Czepiel using the film *Sister Act* starring Whoopi Goldberg to encourage their pupils to "sing up" in Mass. She also remembers her own class making up a song of their own when some of them were nervous about rubella injections:

"It may cause you strife, it may cause you pain, but you're never gonna get German measles again! Rubella! Rubella!"

Overcrowded or not, no-one could deny the historic charm of the Old Hall with its beautiful plasterwork and gilded honour boards. It has been the scene for various celebrations, and has even hosted a wedding reception, on May 12th, 1991, after the marriage of Miss Natalija Lazarewicz of the Science Department to Mr Stojimir Djukic. (Their daughter Aleksia is now a pupil).

Miss Geraldine Brown and Mr. Rhyd Evans at Book Day, October 1992.

The New Hall continued to be the venue for enjoyable events, often involving both staff and pupils dressing up and generally letting their hair down. The staff pantomime was resurrected with new jokes and songs in 1992, and there were some uproarious events for Comic Relief. Often it was the male teachers who were most ready to sacrifice their dignity for charity. Another memory of Bernadette Shortt involves fundraising for the Children in Need appeal:

"One of the funniest sights ever was being taught history by Mr McGurran wearing his wife's Irish dancing dress complete with matching headdress. We made a lot of money for the appeal that year."

This was the same Mr Brendan McGurran who was pictured at a summer fête in the stocks with girls queuing up to throw wet sponges at him, a fate also suffered in their time by Mr Rhyd Evans and Mr Steve Earp. St. Paul's staff have always been ready to have a bit of fun in a good cause, and generations of girls have enjoyed seeing another side of their teachers.

Miss Mary Holland, who was the fête master-planner in the 90s, succeeding Mrs Anne Berry's sterling work in the previous decade, recalls that the annual summer fêtes unified the efforts of staff, pupils, parents and friends of the school.

Sr. Thérèse at fête, 1993.

"It was a fun day, but a busy, tiring one for stall-holders. Preparations began weeks ahead with lots of encouragement and competitions between forms to bring items to sell or create novel games. Toys, gifts and bottles were gathered for the respective tombolas, always money-spinners. Cakes and scones were made for the cream teas. Visiting bands were invited to take part and Irish dancers were always popular participants, with St. Paul's musicians playing their part.

"Guests were invited to open the fête, notably our own Clare Short, Sarah Smart, now a very successful actress, and the M.P. for Edgbaston, Gisela Stuart. Sr. Marie Agnes and Sr. Thérèse also opened the fête after their retirement. The staff were busy; you would see Mrs Holbeche, Sr. Helena and Miss Eastwood serving teas; Mrs Hodgson and Mrs Mulry selling cakes; Madame Laurent, Mrs Johnson and Mrs Durrani making pancakes and waffles, while Sr. Hilary, Mrs Jinks and Mrs Adams manned the tombolas. Miss Wilson and Mr Cox were the experts on the plant stall; Mrs Brennan and Mrs Wynne would be hidden among the second-hand books, while Mrs Meyrick, Mrs Harris and their husbands were cooking hamburgers and hot dogs, not forgetting Miss Armstrong and her chip machine!

Mr McGurran in the Stocks.

"The fête day was nearly always fine and was only forced inside two or three times in twenty years. It was always a happy day, and it was so good to see everyone working together for the benefit of the school."

The decade of the 90s was not however without sadness and bereavement. In June, 1992 the school was shocked at the very sudden death of Michelle O'Donoghue, a Sixth Former who was just about to begin A-level examinations when she succumbed to a previously unsuspected heart condition. A white rose was planted in the Convent courtyard in her memory. Later that year, in October, the death was announced of Maureen Gaffney who had left school only in 1991, after achieving good A-level grades. In spite of suffering painful bone cancer, Maureen achieved her Gold Duke of Edinburgh Award just a fortnight before she died. She was a junior instructor with the Young Firefighters, and went under their auspices on a special Duke of Edinburgh expedition to Australia, in 1990, for which she and her friend Mary Power spent weeks raising money. One Friday afternoon a fire engine complete with "Simon snorkel" hoist arrived at school, and astonished classes at the

Clare Short, Roger Browning, Gerard Coghlan, School Fête, 1996.

front of the building were treated to the sight of Maureen, Mary and Sister Agnes rising slowly, and with great dignity on Sister's part anyway, to the height of the first floor classrooms and above.

In May, 1993, a large number of staff and pupils attended the funeral of Catherine Kenny, who left school in 1988 and was fondly remembered as a really brave and lively character. She suffered from cystic fibrosis, entailing daily physiotherapy and many spells in hospital, but never allowed this to dampen her own spirits or those of anyone around her. Catherine even gained her Bronze Duke of Edinburgh Award while in school, with the help of Cathy Hynes, who carried her on their expedition when she became too tired to walk.

Very shortly afterwards the school suffered a great shock when Mrs Eleanor Gay, Head of History for 13 years, and a Sixth form tutor, died suddenly just as she was about to set out for school one Monday morning. She was an inspiring teacher with a great love of her subject, often using drama in her lessons to encourage pupils to get a real grasp of historical events and characters. She organised lively "mock" elections

Summer Fête, 1998. Mary Holland, Gisela Stuart, M.P.,
Roger Browning and Dr. Gerard Coghlan.

which involved the school in listening to candidates' speeches and voting on real issues. As well as being a good friend to many colleagues, Eleanor Gay was also particularly encouraging to younger staff in her role as mentor to newly qualified teachers. A tree was planted in her memory in the front garden, close to the main entrance.

The school continued throughout this time to be in the forefront, along with others in the Birmingham Catholic Partnership, of educational innovation, especially in the field of Information Technology. One development which caused some apprehension was the introduction of the OFSTED system of inspections. There was quite a lot of time to prepare for the first one, but the process gave rise to a great deal of paperwork and nervous speculation, as no-one really knew what to expect. It was a cold, dark January day in 1994 when the team of inspectors (all nine of them!) arrived, but things went well, and the Senior Staff were told at the end of the week that not only did they have a cake, but there was icing on it, and all they needed were a few cherries for the top! It was a great relief that the inspection was over, but many

Maureen Gaffney, Mary Power, Sr. Agnes about to ascend, 1990.

staff commented on the reaction felt after a long period of stress, and the effort needed to buckle down to, and survive the rest of a busy spring term.

In July, 1994, two long-serving and influential members of staff retired. Mrs Margaret O'Brien (née Bryan) had been in charge of Business Studies since 1980, having attended an Old Girls' Reunion and been head-hunted by Sister Agnes when she was discovered to be a teacher of Commercial subjects. She recalls, "I joined the staff on the same day as Mrs Holbeche and, as we met in the cloakroom at the end of the day, we both felt we should say thank you to Sr. Agnes for letting us join the school – it was such a delightful atmosphere – and this never changed over the next fourteen years."

The other retiree was Mrs Dilys Meyrick, Head of Sixth Form and Modern Language teacher, who remembered "the spring day in 1960 as I walked along Vernon Road, smartly dressed for interview in suit, hat and gloves, wondering what Catholics were like! I remember my first sight of Sister Josephine, then Sister Ethelbert, dressed in traditional habit, and recall not knowing if I should curtsey or shake hands!"

90th Anniversary celebrations. Dawn Casserly, Liz Plummer, Kathy Westwood and Marian Dick.

Former pupils and colleagues will remember Dilys Meyrick as a very lively teacher with a great sense of humour, who built up strong links with commerce and industry through her work in establishing the Careers Department. Her husband John was always ready to help out at school functions and events, from lending his powerful voice in music productions to officiating at the barbecue stall at the summer fête.

As in earlier periods there has been great continuity of staff. The 1990s saw the departure of some long-serving teachers, like Mr Tony White, Head of Maths from 1973 to 1995, who has continued to be very involved with the musical life of the school, and still teaches recorder groups. Others who retired in the 90s were Mrs Simpson, Head of English from 1972 to 1993, then Pastoral Co-ordinator, and Mrs Harris, also from the English Department and long-standing Head of Year 7, Mrs Johnson, Mrs Steward and Madame Laurent from Modern Languages, Miss Holland, Deputy Head and Classics, and Mr Mellor (magpie-slayer and now full-time farmer), Head of Geography. Two notable "school-leavers" who never really retired at all are Sister Helena (English, R.E. and Exam secretary) and Sister Hilary (Classics, Library and everything, really). Sister Helena left St. Paul's in July, 1999 and the following year went off to Rustenburg in South Africa to teach at Selly Park School (one of the Sisters' many outposts and now a valued international link for St. Paul's). Sister is a keen photographer and makes the most of the opportunities she now has to capture exotic scenery and wildlife.

Dawn Casserly, Deputy Head pays tribute to Sister Helena. "She taught me R.E. but also so much about faith, life and goodness. There was never a question she would not answer and she gave us the confidence to express our opinions free from condemnation. She created such a spirit of openness and intellectual honesty in lessons. She instilled in me the confidence to seek the truth… And in her words, 'not to be a sheep!'"

As if this were not enough to prove that Sisters never retire, Sister Hilary went off to study in Ireland for a year after leaving school, but returned to spend almost as much time as before at St. Paul's, assisting particularly with R.E. and Chaplaincy work as well as Latin. She has also given a great deal of time to Romania. It is well-known that Sister has an encyclopaedic knowledge of former pupils and maintains extensive links with generations of St. Paul's girls, who regard her with great affection as embodying the school's caring spirit along with a dashing energy that is all her own.

During the years from 1991–1999 Mrs Helen Peters held the post of Deputy Head. Helen was a pupil at school in the 1970s, a talented musician and sportswoman. One Remembrance Day Assembly was enhanced by the notes of Helen's trumpet floating down into the Hall from the windows above, sounding the Last Post. As Deputy, Helen switched effortlessly between business suit and tracksuit, even finding time to resume debates with her old sparring partner, Mr Mellor. She left to devote more time to her young family, the elder of whom, Roberta, is now a pupil.

In October, 1998 St. Paul's celebrated its ninetieth anniversary. Among other events there was a special assembly narrating the history of the school through the decades, in music, dance and drama. The staff dressed up (as usual they could not be stopped!) in the style of 1908, and the pupils adopted costumes of whichever decade they chose. Sister Hilary recorded the novelty of wearing the old-style nun's habit:

"Tripping over one's skirts, hanging oneself on door-handles with dangling rosary beads, one's sight confined to tunnel vision, isn't exactly conducive to an air of elegance! However, we were frequently told how much younger we looked – no white hair to be seen! So perhaps the designers of the old habit had achieved something after all! And it was great fun."

Mrs Dunne took a lesson 1908-style, with her class reciting the alphabet backwards, proclaiming the two-times table and copying pothooks to symbolise the letter 'S'. All this proceeded to the accompaniment of severe remarks from the teacher about cleanliness and godliness. Perhaps the watching late twentieth century audience realised they were not so badly off after all.

90th Anniversary Assembly. Mrs B. Dunne takes a lesson 1908 style.

There was also a traditional drill lesson (Miss Liz Plummer in a 1920s style bathing suit), and recollections from each decade accompanied by appropriate music, from *Pack up your Troubles* through to Sting and the Spice Girls. The assembly finished with the traditional prayers and the *Hymn to St. Paul*, all the more poignant because it was known by then that Sr. Thérèse would be leaving at the end of that term to become Superior-General of the Order, and that, for the first time in ninety years, there would not be a St. Paul's Sister as Head. Sister Hilary wrote at the time, "Many staff asked us sadly afterwards whether the sisters would still be here for the Centenary. We could only answer that it is in the hands of God."

Happily, at the centenary the Sisters are still very much involved, with Sister Thérèse and Sister Jean Shedden on the Governing Body, Sister Ursula very active in the English and Special Needs Departments, and Sister Hilary herself continuing to be an energetic presence every day in school, and particularly active in the Chaplaincy sphere.

Nevertheless, Sister Thérèse's election to the office of Superior brought a sense of loss as well as joy. She combined most effectively two styles of leadership not always found in one person: a talent for methodical organisation and management together with a capacity for warm personal relationships which greatly uplifted and motivated staff and pupils.

Sister Thérèse continued Sister Agnes's mission of upholding traditional standards while embracing the best of the many educational initiatives of the time. She was a very modern Head, characterised in the ninetieth anniversary assembly as wearing a safety helmet and carrying a clipboard. Following the relaxation of dress conventions in the Congregation, she was the first to dispense with the headdress. Sarah Simmons remembers the shock this caused on the morning she entered the assembly hall bareheaded; "Rumours were rife: she'd left the convent and run off with a priest!"

Top left: Senior Management Team, 1999. Top right: St. Paul's Old Girls on the staff, 1999.
Bottom left: Duke of Edinburgh Award Winners with Lord Mayor.
Bottom right: Staff, 1993–94.

No-one though was ever in doubt of the authority present in her petite figure. "Leaving St. Paul's in 1994 we all brought in markers to sign our shirts… Sister Thérèse had other ideas however, and marched us all into the hall for a shirt inspection! Many girls were issued with replacement shirts and their own whisked away!"

The staff's abiding image, though, was sparked off by something Sister herself once read to us, concerning the flight of geese and the fact that there is always a 'lead' goose in the front of the V-formation. Thereafter in staff entertainments and skits, she was Mother Goose leading her flock through trials and triumphs, Ofsteds and off-days, always with humanity, humour and vision for the school.

Chapter 13

PARENTS' ASSOCIATION

On April 4th, 1966, a meeting was held to discuss the formation of a parents' association, and a committee was elected with a representation of fathers and mothers from each year group. At the same meeting, Alderman Sir Francis Griffin spoke about plans for the reorganisation of schools in the city, a topic that would continue to be hotly debated for at least another eight years.

The Association's first major activity was support for the school fête in July, and over the next few years the organisation of this function became one of their principal activities. The money raised from these and other enterprises paid for, among other things, tennis courts, the organ and window curtains in the New Hall and the four large mirrors in the 'old' entrance hall.

The Parents' Association also organised a wide variety of social activities including dances, talks, cheese and wine evenings, Polish, Indian and Scottish themed evenings, as well as theatre visits and outings.

At first, Sister Josephine chaired the meetings, but at some stage in Sister Agnes's time, the Chair was taken by a parent. Mrs Siekierski was an early member and treasurer of long standing, and other offices were held at various times by Mr Banner, Mr Dudgeon, Mr Elcock, Mr Kevin Askew, Mr Graham Evans and Mr O'Dell. At a later stage in the 1980s, the Association became the Parent Teacher Association, and finally the Parents, Teachers and Friends Association, in which form it continued to flourish. Mrs Morby as Deputy Head was the main school link in the Association, followed in the late 1980s and 1990s by Miss Holland. In addition to the Head Teachers, other staff involved have been Mrs Maureen May, Mrs Inge Durrani, Mrs Jan Wynne, Miss Judith Allan and Miss Mary Byers. The school's office staff have made a particularly notable contribution, with Mrs Christine Kirby, Mrs Maureen Leese and Mrs Sue Redmond organising raffles and a Disco for the Year 6 pupils to introduce them to St. Paul's. Mrs Wendy Gamsby co-ordinated the PTFA contribution to the Flower Festival.

As well as fund raising and socialising, parents were happy to help the school in practical ways. Mr Roger Browning, Treasurer and then Chairman in the 1990s, remembers that the biggest project undertaken was to smarten up and redecorate the toilet and cloakroom areas in the prefabs which were looking very tired at the time. Other projects carried out included repairing various outbuildings around the school, repairing the grotto and creating its garden.

Roger recalls that it was at the meeting arranged by the first OFSTED inspectors to meet parents that he really began to appreciate just how much parents cared for and supported St. Paul's. "The inspector was in for a surprise, as he admitted at the end of the meeting. The Hall was full for a start, a first for the inspector. Secondly he was quizzed as to his background, qualifications and whether he would appreciate the very strong Catholic ethos of the school. As far as we were concerned St. Paul's was already an excellent school, so why did we need an inspection?"

He recalls the hard work that went into the summer fête, and the formidable task of co-ordination that fell to Miss Holland, though as he says many hands made light work of the stallholding and clearing-up at the end. Roger continues, "Although the PTFA raised many thousands of pounds and helped fund many projects and extras, what was equally important was the fun we had. There were quizzes, dances, fêtes and many more events. If I had a favourite it would be the annual cricket match between staff and parents. This was held at the Pickwick Club in Moseley. Most of the arrangements fell on Liz Plummer of the P.E. staff, and it was her father Peter who umpired. It wasn't just the P.E. staff who played as most departments were represented, including Sister Thérèse.

"Apart from enjoying the company of like-minded families and the interaction with the staff, my enduring memories were the many ways in which we worked together to enhance the education and opportunities for our daughters. The PTFA was never just about raising additional money to fund those extras that the education budgets couldn't run to. It was, as with the Trinity, about being as one, the staff, governors and parents seeking to help educate and support our daughters."

Roger Browning's successor as Chair of the PTFA was Mrs Linda Conlon. In her first welcome speech to new parents she related how at first she had felt scared about going to meetings and speaking up. The following extract shows how confident she became!

"Everyone made me feel at ease and then somehow they conned me into becoming CHAIR! The information gained at these meetings is great, because you ask your daughter what's going on in school and they will tell you NOTHING. So come along and find out for yourself.

"I have a piece of advice for you; go and buy a new A to Z, or get Satnav, or the latest bus timetable, because your daughter's newest, bestest friend will live on the other side of Birmingham. Trust me, I have three daughters who came or come to this school and a Mum!"

Under Linda's leadership and that of her successor, Mr Michael Stephenson, the PTFA have continued to support the school with Quiz nights, Irish nights, Barbecues, Race nights, Skittles Nights and a successful 50–50 Club. They have paid for new and much needed curtains for the hall and stage, decoration of the dining room, garages for storage, screens, laptops and projectors. They also help serve refreshments at school events and Parents' evenings. As Linda Conlon said, "We can always rely on Miss Whelan to let us know about the next project. But we think they're worth it!"

In 2008 the PTFA will be helping out at different events planned for the Centenary. They are a flourishing organisation, and well exemplify Roger Browning's description of their being an integral part of the school's mission to educate and support their daughters.

Chapter 14

LOOKING BACK AND FORWARD
(1999–2008)

For a term after Sister Thérèse's departure, the post of Acting Head was ably filled by Miss Mary Holland, Deputy and old girl of the school. In April, 1999, the school's first lay Head Teacher took up her position. She is Miss Angela Whelan, who already had strong connections to St. Paul's through her own schooldays at Cardinal Wiseman School in Coventry where Sister Thérèse had taught, and where her Headmistress was Sister Francis Clare Aylward, for many years a governor at St. Paul's and a great friend to the school. Miss Whelan is another strong leader whose energy and enthusiasm have powered St. Paul's into the twenty-first century, and another period of considerable innovation and development.

Miss Angela Whelan,
Head 1999 to present.

When recently some of the longer serving staff were asked about the changes and developments in their fields, some interesting reflections emerged.

The Science Department's accommodation has been greatly extended over the years, sometimes with unforeseen results, like the waterfall that cascaded down the corridor wall in the Chemistry Lab when the two new laboratories were built above it. "The wooden floor warped so much," Miss Sowter remembers, "that we couldn't open the door for three months and had to come into the lab via the computer room."

Mrs Lesley Payne, who has been in the Department for over thirty years, has watched this expansion. Now, as Head of Department, having succeeded Mr Stephen Cox, she is in charge of seven science classrooms, a staff office, science computer room and two well-equipped prep. rooms.

Miss Dobie notes that over the years many of the more "interesting" chemicals have been removed from school science labs. "We are no longer allowed, because of 'H&S' to 'play' with mercury, or to create mini volcanoes with ammonium dichromate. The emphasis now is much more on learning chemical ideas through real 'stories' about how chemistry works."

Mr Holmes adds that Physics has changed dramatically with the inclusion of material from quantum mechanics, cosmology and relativity. It is less dry and esoteric than formerly, and now computers give the power to log data that would have been impossible previously.

Some things last though; Miss Sowter points out that there are still quite a few solid oak stools in the Chemistry Lab dating from 1954. "They've lasted rather better than the stools we bought ten years ago that are falling apart now."

The prefabricated buildings erected after the fire could, before their demolition have also been described as 'falling apart', but despite these unpromising surrounding, there has been no diminution in the success of the English Department, going from strength to strength under its new leader, Ms Maggie Stilliard. They continue to have outstanding results at A-level, GCSE and in SATS and have a leading role in mentoring PGCE students. The Public Speaking Competition, a tradition begun by the present author, provides a challenging platform for budding orators as well as entertainment, and there are more opportunities than ever for theatre visits, locally and to Stratford.

Computers are now used in every department. Mr Chris Guy has been in the forefront of development virtually since the beginning of IT provision. He and long-serving technician Simon Green continue to provide valuable expertise and assistance to other staff in this area. Mr Guy recalls that "in 1982 the school took delivery of its first computer, as part of a Government programme to place a computer in every secondary school. It was housed in a converted cloakroom, which is now Miss

Casserly's office. The big black box was used by pupils studying O-level Computer Studies. It would require forty thousand of those black boxes to produce the power of just one of the many computers in school today.

"Things moved on quickly with the first network of twelve stations being installed in 1987, with the then massive storage capacity of 20 megabytes shared between all 900 users… over the years the network rapidly expanded, and today the computer system covers almost every room in the school; over 300 machines are now an essential part of running this institution."

One example is the School Library, where all resources are logged on to computer. The Library these days is a cheerful and active place, where Mrs Jinks and Mrs Adams, in addition to all the usual library support, run a flourishing stationery shop and organise competitions and quizzes.

The Geography Department has continued to reach out to a wide variety of places, both nationally and internationally. In addition to the established visits to Ludlow, Stratford and Stansfeld, there are opportunities for residential courses at Scarborough, and European links with countries like Finland. The Head of Department, Mrs Mary Atterbury, was seconded several years ago to teach in the Cayman Islands, only to be followed there by Hurricane Ivan, which caused such destruction that she was forced to make an unscheduled return. Her department flourishes and is particularly skilled at mentoring graduate students, having successfully seen three through the Graduate Teaching Programme.

Modern Languages too led by Mrs Jo Wakelin has branched out and now offers French, Spanish and Italian. Trips abroad continue to be a popular feature, and there is a new tradition of a European Languages Day, which involves tasting delicious food and even participating in a master class in Salsa dancing. Spanish has now worked its way through the years to A-level-standard; one 2007–08 student, Alice Gomez, who comes from a Spanish family background, says, "I find the A-level course interesting and challenging, as it requires you to do more independent research and go beyond your comfort zone in terms of vocabulary."

Visitors to the upper floor above the Head's and secretaries' offices are now greeted by a dazzling and regularly changing exhibition of the Art Department's work. Under the leadership of Mrs Judi Lanchester and her colleague Mrs Linda Arnold-Morgan, there have been many innovations including the introduction of three dimensional studies using chicken-wire, wood and felts. Mrs Lanchester came to the department in 1988 and has established a tradition of taking students from Birmingham City University to work in the Department. Over the years 30 Art students have helped to feed in fresh ideas and concepts, and to facilitate workshops in etching, plaster-casting and photography.

Now the work of three of St. Paul's Art students is on display in the Parliament building in Dublin, and the school has featured on Central TV, and even on YOUTUBE, through the department's involvement with the Birmingham Re-Dress project, where students produced fashion concepts and dresses using recycled material.

Design and Technology is another relatively new and exciting department under the leadership of Mrs Liz Holbeche. Part of this is Food Technology, led by Mrs Bridget Mulry. They occupy rooms between the Art department and science labs on the first floor of the "new" block, which was the last area on the upper floor to be filled in, and opened in November, 1998. As part of work linked to the centenary, Bridget charted the history of her subject for the students, pointing out that it was first known as Cookery, became Domestic Science at some time after the war, metamorphosed into Home Economics at some stage in the 1960s, and was then subsumed into Technology. Girls still very much enjoy cooking, and recently they have enjoyed demonstrations by professional chefs. Another popular event was the Parent-Daughter day which saw mothers and fathers cooking alongside their girls.

Downstairs Mr Earp's students are busy assembling various products with wood, metal and other resistant materials amid a cheerful clatter of machinery. An AS-level course in textiles has begun in 2007, being already successful at GCSE. Another very popular course which grew out of Home Economics and Science, independently of Technology, is Child Development, led by Mrs Djukic.

A curriculum area which has developed beyond recognition from the early days of drill in the hall is Physical Education, which now successfully runs GCSE and A-level courses. The school always enjoyed success in traditional sports like hockey and tennis, latterly under long-serving Head of Department Tina Luesley. Now Miss Caroline Wright and her team have built on this with a wide variety of activities in lessons and as extra-curricular provision. The Year 10 Netball team won the Torquay national tournament in 2007. The Basketball team is going well too, unbeaten in the Autumn Term of 2007.

Football is proving very popular, with the Year 8 and Year 10 teams each winning their sections of the Aston Power League. Another hit has been Gaelic football. The team's first Head Coach Louise McCauley remembers, "On many an evening after school Years 10 and 11 could be seen bouncing and kicking a ball with great enjoyment." The girls finished second in their very first tournament. Now Gaelic

Left: Assault Challenge – Field group at Blackwell, 2006.
Right: Netball Team, 2007.

football is an established part of the curriculum, along with basketball, rowing, badminton, orienteering, rounders, step aerobics and gymnastics, among other sports. P.E. uniform is now a navy tracksuit bearing the school logo – but they still wear those bright yellow socks!

Not only have the established curriculum subjects been brought right up to date, there are now opportunities to study and acquire experience which were quite unthought of in 1958 much less 1908. For instance the school has been committed to work-related learning since the 1980s when Mrs O'Brien established a programme of work experience. Miss Gina Hirst, who is now in charge of this area, lists the variety of activities.

"Our students were introduced to the rigours of the interview process early on, with a programme of practice interviews, conducted by professional interviewers. There are Careers evenings for Year 9, hectic and demanding "Quo Vadis days" for Year 11, and most recently the "Catwalk Experience" in which girls had one day to form themselves into business teams to design, make and promote evening gowns."

New subjects at A-level include Psychology, which, despite being introduced as recently as 2003, by Mrs Michele Darke, is now one of the most popular courses, continuing under Mrs Craddock's leadership. An earlier, but equally popular introduction from 1987 has been Sociology, begun by Mrs Yvonne Brennan, ably assisted by Miss McCauley. Consistently outstanding results have been achieved. The present curriculum leader in Sociology is Miss Beth Tibbits, who was chosen as West Midlands Regional Finalist in the National Teaching Awards of 2007, enthusiastically supported by her students and colleagues.

St. Paul's was one of the first schools, in 2002, to appoint a Learning Mentor, Miss Louise Morgan, with the aim of removing barriers to learning. She works with students who need help with curriculum content, or where there have been difficulties in relationships with other pupils or teachers. Miss Morgan is training a team of "peer mentors" so that students can help and support others.

There are also now many more non-teaching staff, from laboratory technicians to classroom assistants, at present numbering eight. Under the leadership of Miss Mary Byers, Assistant Head with responsibility for Special Educational Needs, they provide support for pupils and their emotional, physical, academic or behavioural well-being. One pupil who came to St. Paul's in 2002, diagnosed as having Down's Syndrome, is now due to go to college, and speaks fondly of everyone who has supported her. "I'm going to miss St. Paul's," says Lorna Sylvester, "I've loved it here."

The secretarial staff especially have grown in number since the days of Sister Gertrude or Sister Kevin manning the office on her own; they are now a highly efficient team with individual roles housed in a suite of rooms. Mrs Sheila Pellowe is Personal Assistant to the Head, succeeding such well-remembered figures as Roxie Holt and Breda Hanley. Now there is a Finance Officer, Mrs Jovic, a separate Reprographics room, manned full-time, and the roles of the office staff include assisting with managing support staff, work experience placements, assessment Management, UCAS applications, pastoral administration and public examination entries, to name but a few.

In all this innovation it is noticeable how often teachers have developed their expertise in fields quite different from those in which they began their career. Mrs May, for instance, a well-loved Head of Year 7 for many years now, began her career at St. Paul's as Head of P.E., returned later as an English teacher, and is now in charge of Key Stage 3 (Years 7–9!) She is also a fantastically successful fundraiser, for Romania and for the numerous other causes the school supports. Miss McCauley effortlessly combined History and Sociology with Gaelic Football and the pastoral care of a year group through the trials of Key Stage 4. Miss Sowter, in charge of Chemistry for many years has turned her hand to co-ordinating the Gifted and Talented programme, while managing to keep up what a departing Sixth former once called her "ongoing romance with Shakespeare." Mrs Jan Wynne combines English teaching and being Head of Year 8 with training ITT students and mentoring newly qualified teachers, while Mrs Margaret Sutherland has a long and successful record of teaching Maths as well as co-ordinating Vocational Education and Key Skills. Mrs Trevor (Geography), Mrs Seery (History) and Mrs Canavan (English) are all Heads of Year. There is no member of staff who does not have at least two roles, those of subject teacher and form tutor, and some have many more!

In January 2003 the school's third OFSTED inspection took place. The judgment of the inspectors gave staff and pupils as much pleasure as that long ago report of 1908 did to Mother Emelia and her colleagues. St. Paul's was judged "an excellent school. Good and much very good teaching is promoting very good achievement and well above average standards in national tests and external examinations… excellent leadership, with strong support from governors, ensures that the school has a distinctive ethos in which pupils are provided with a high quality education." The inspectors also highlighted "the excellent provision for spiritual and moral development which provides pupils with a securely based value system, and makes a significant contribution to their personal development."

The only concern for a school on receiving such an accolade must be, "Can we keep this up when the inspectors come again?" The inspectors' visit in February, 2007 yielded the following report: "St. Paul's School for Girls is an outstanding school with a distinctive Catholic ethos in which values are shared and careful attention is given to meeting the needs of, and developing, the whole person." In a letter to the pupils telling them about their findings the inspectors said, "You clearly enjoy the time you spend at school, even though many of you have to set off very early in the morning to arrive on time… Your head teacher and her senior team have excellent systems to identify when you might be in need of additional academic or pastoral help and teachers and other staff provide you with exceptional levels of support and guidance."

In 2006, another very long-serving and much-loved teacher, Miss Claire Eastwood, retired, having headed the R.E. Department for 32 years, and taught at St. Paul's for 37. No-one who attended a School Mass in all those years will fail to have been inspired by the beautiful liturgy she created with her poetic talent. Masses and assemblies would be planned as much as six months in advance of the event. Bernadette Shortt pays tribute to the effect she had.

"Miss Eastwood was the queen when it came to public speaking. You could hear the excitement in the assembly hall when she took the stage. She really made us howl with laughter with her speeches based on the song 'Living next door to Alice', and when she brought in her beloved dog Megan."

At Miss Eastwood's retirement Mass, her successor, Miss Margaret Czepiel, spoke of her "self-sacrifice and utter dedication to the pupils of St. Paul's, whom she encouraged to strive for excellence, since 'A is for acceptable!'" On a lighter note, and echoing Miss Eastwood's famous penchant for alliteration, she dubbed her "our

Music Recital, 2007.

Cookstown Cyclone, Tyrone Tornado, Clint, Boss, Honky Tonk Woman, but above all the Anam Cara and soul friend to so many."

Miss Liz Plummer, a former pupil who went on to teach P.E. at St. Paul's, recalled an incident from her Sixth form days in the late 70s. "In our R.E. group we had a star pupil, Susan Docherty, who always got A's. Miss Eastwood was forever asking why the rest of us could not produce work like Susan's!... When Miss Eastwood set us an assignment for the Easter holiday, Susan produced her essay and I took it and photocopied it fifteen times. We then wrote our names on top of each essay, wrapped them up and presented them to Miss Eastwood – after all she had asked us to produce work like Susan's. We then all took cover!" (Susan Docherty returned to present the prizes at Awards Evening, 2007. She is now Head of Theology, Philosophy and Religious Education at Newman University College).

Sarah Cahill remembers an R.E. lesson from when OFSTED visited in 2003. "Miss Eastwood wanted to show the inspector how much we knew. She began asking us many questions as a recap and while she was doing this she picked up a wooden mallet that had been used to put a display up. As the lesson went on, when she asked us questions as individuals she would point the mallet at us. We all thought it was funny but kept our cool in front of the inspector – however he did see the funny side at the end of the lesson!"

The report of the Inspectors on the R.E. department was, as usual, glowing.

At her retirement Mass Claire Eastwood was presented with the Archbishop's Medal for Service; the same recognition was given to Mrs Maria Hodgson, retiring after 27 years. She was described as "the multi-talented, multi-faceted and multi-tasking Technology Teacher, Head of Year, Exam Secretary, Special Needs Co-ordinator and Assistant Head Teacher... A woman of substance." In the culminating years of her career, Mrs Hodgson was particularly involved in the very 21st Century task of analysing educational data and helping staff to use it to advance pupils' achievement and improve results. She carried on work both in this area and in the pastoral care of girls which had been developed by Mrs Yvonne Brennan, another well-

Top: Biology Field Trip, 2006.
Bottom: Group at Ogwen Cottage, 2006.

loved and much respected teacher and Deputy Head from 2001 till 2005 when she left to become Head Teacher of St. Augustine's School in Redditch.

Like Helen Goodwin, with whom she had earlier worked very closely, Yvonne Brennan has a great capacity for grasping and disseminating all that is most useful in current educational thinking, as well as great sensitivity to pupils and colleagues and tremendous dedication to the school's mission of promoting the graceful growth of the whole person. Along with Anne Berry, Head of Mathematics and Angela Whelan, she put a great deal of work into the school's successful bid for Specialist Status. Yvonne also developed the school's extremely successful A-level programme in Sociology, as well as having served as a Staff Governor. The school owes her much gratitude.

Archbishop Couve de Murville, Mrs Morby, Miss Eastwood, 1988.

Among new arrivals in the staff room during recent years have been several more former pupils, or, as some don't mind being called, Old Girls. An unofficial sub-group on the staff these days is the SPOGOTS: St. Paul's Old Girls on the Staff! They are sufficient in number to have attracted media attention both from Central TV and the local press, and include among their number Deputy Head Teacher Dawn Casserly, recognised by all as a tower of strength in the school's pastoral and management systems as well as the R.E. department (yet still finding the energy to be a passionate Aston Villa supporter!) One department which has particularly benefited from this revolving door movement is History, headed by Mrs Shinead Coyle (née Rock), with Miss Julie Mason (Assistant Head Teacher) and Mrs Sarah Shelton (née Simmons) supporting her.

Fund-raising has continued to play a big part in school life, and been the source of a lot of fun. In addition to supporting well-established local and national charities such as Father Hudson's, St. Mary's Hospice, Acorns Hospice, the Edward Trust, the Fireside Project, Save the Children and Cafod, a great deal of money has been raised for Romania. Since 2002, the school has made special efforts for Breast Cancer Care, involving sponsored walking round the reservoir by all the pupils. Girls were particularly keen to do this after several members of staff and relatives received treatment for the disease. In 2006 donations by the school to all charities totalled close on £15,000. Now a very large effort is being made to raise money for Freedom Park in South Africa, brought to the school's notice by our international link with Selly Park School in Rustenburg.

Freedom Park is a squatter camp next to the platinum mines near Rustenburg, in the North West Province of South Africa. Conditions are very poor and there are a great number of sufferers from HIV/AIDS, as well as children orphaned by disease and poverty. The school is supporting the Tapologo programme set up by the Archdiocese of Rustenburg to provide care and education for such children, and to enrol them in schools and skills development schemes. Over the years from 2006 to 2008, each class has planned to adopt a child from Africa as their special project. In September, 2006, a sponsored walk raised £6000 for the cause, and it looks certain this amount will be exceeded in the following years. In 2007, in addition to raising funds through the annual sponsored walk and other events, over £2000 was raised as

Sisters and St. Paul's Old Girls on the staff, 1999.

119

Left: Miss Whelan and Miss Casserly celebrate on Demolition Day.
Right: Senior Managers and staff from Selly Park School, South Africa.

a donation to Freedom Park in memory of Sofia Cozzi, a very popular and talented Year 12 student who tragically fell victim to Sudden Death Syndrome during the summer holiday.

Pilgrimages to Lourdes have continued, with Years 11, 12 and 13 making regular trips in their May holidays to assist the sick in the baths and visiting the shrines, while Year 7 travel there at Easter. A new tradition is springing up of regular trips to the First World War battlefields of Belgium, to enhance work in English and History. In addition to a huge variety of visits and field trips, there have been excursions to France and more recently to Spain, since Spanish is now a fast-developing and popular part of the Modern Languages curriculum.

Sarah Cahill, Deputy Head Girl in 2004, comments: "St. Paul's gave me the opportunity to go abroad for the first time without my family. We visited the battlefields and graves in France and Belgium to support our GCSE work. I remember feeling very emotional about the loss of life that had occurred. Although you can learn about it in the classroom nothing is better than experiencing the effects of war first hand. That weekend was also the weekend that Atomic Kitten's *Whole Again* was released. I'm sure that by the time we got back to Birmingham the teachers were sick of hearing the song – although we made a very good choir on the coach!"

In September, 2005, the school was awarded Specialist Status in Maths and Computing, after a great deal of hard work on preparing a bid and securing sponsorship. Under Mrs Berry's leadership, the Maths Department has seen exciting developments, with special events such as Code Breaking Days, Murder Mystery Days and Maths challenges. There are also workshops for parents. As well as promoting the teaching of Mathematics and ICT in the school itself, this involves St. Paul's in links with feeder primary schools and the wider community. In addition to the connection made some years ago with St. Paul's Secondary School in Greenhills, Dublin, the school has built on the Sisters' traditional links with South Africa by choosing as its international connection Selly Park Secondary School in Rustenburg. The project was launched by a visit from Miss Whelan to South Africa where she met Sister Christine, the Head Teacher and her staff. She reported that "the St. Paul's shield is evident everywhere, and the school field is called Birmingham." A further visit from St. Paul's staff has already been made, and teachers from Rustenburg visited Vernon Road in summer, 2007.

Another teacher, Miss Anne Wright of the ICT department, was able to visit Los Angeles to be trained in the delivery of the Oracle computer programme. Other links have been with the Fireside Day Centre in Birmingham, where St. Paul's staff have run courses on literacy skills and Internet use. Work on computer skills has also gone on at the Birmingham Brushstrokes Project, and at the Irish Welfare Centre, helping members of the over-60s group to become familiar with basic e-mailing and internet use.

All of this has made St. Paul's an even more exciting place as it moves towards the celebration of its centenary. In June, 2007, a particularly welcome piece of news was received from the Local Education Authority. A constant refrain over most of the last century has been the lack of classroom space, despite all the various alterations and additions. The prefabricated classrooms installed after the fire of 1974 had an estimated life of ten years and yet some of them stood for over thirty years, leaking and draughty in winter, stifling in summer. Their replacement was the only area for improvement that inspectors could suggest in the last two OFSTEDs.

Now the school has been awarded a grant towards a new building to be erected at the back of the convent, on the site of the oldest prefab buildings. This was due in no small part to the tireless determination of Angela Whelan in lobbying various agencies and generally keeping the school's desperate need for new premises in the forefront of the authorities' minds! Once again, although there is a grant, a substantial part of the cost will be borne by the Congregation of the Sisters of St. Paul. Plans have been drawn up for a three storey building on which work began in September, 2007. The demolition of most of the prefabricated buildings was a red-letter day. As Miss Whelan says, "The Walls of Jericho have come down – metaphorically speaking." The

Top: 17th December 2007: Rededication of the Foundation Stone, Miss Whelan, Sr. Thérèse and Archbishop Vincent Nichols with pupils. Bottom: 17th December 2007 – Founder's Day. Mrs Mary Browning, Chair of Governors, leads prayers for the rededication of the Foundation Stone laid on 17th December, 1907.

event was photographed and the wonderful sight captured of Miss Whelan and Miss Casserly dancing with glee! Already the classrooms have been designated with the names of the former Headmistresses and teaching Sisters, as well as an ICT suite named after the Congregation's Founder, Mother Genevieve Dupuis. The new building is eagerly awaited by the English Department among others, having been housed for many years in the prefabs with no modern technology and less than salubrious working conditions (P10 in particular never smelt the same after the burst pipe and flood in 1993!)

Many plans are now in place for the school's celebration of its centenary, including special gatherings for former pupils and staff in June, 2008. A ceremonial re-laying of the Foundation Stone was enacted on December 17th, 2007, with a Mass and Blessing conducted by Archbishop Vincent Nichols. Everything is being recorded and photographed for posterity! So, just as it did in 1907 and 1908, Vernon Road resounds to the builders' hammers, and indeed much more modern equipment, as the school goes forward into its next hundred years, sustained by the prayers, good wishes and memories of its many cohorts of past and present pupils and staff. Most would agree that though the school motto, *Omnibus Omnia*, All things to all People, is an ambitious one and notoriously difficult to pull off, St. Paul's has made a pretty good effort to realise it over the last century. Long may it continue!

INDEX